Penguin Critical Studies

Hamlet

Sydney Bolt was educated̶ ̶ ̶
Cambridge University, wh̶ ̶ ̶
English on return from six̶ ̶ ̶
returned to India for te̶ ̶ ̶ ̶ ̶
Cambridgeshire College of Arts and Technology. He has written books
and articles on James Joyce, poetry and the teaching of English.

Penguin Critical Studies
Advisory Editor:
Bryan Loughrey

William Shakespeare

Hamlet

Sydney Bolt

Penguin Books

PENGUIN BOOKS

Published by the Penguin Group
Penguin Books Ltd, 27 Wrights Lane, London W8 5TZ, England
Penguin Putnam Inc., 375 Hudson Street, New York, New York 10014, USA
Penguin Books Australia Ltd, Ringwood, Victoria, Australia
Penguin Books Canada Ltd, 10 Alcorn Avenue, Toronto, Ontario, Canada M4V 3B2
Penguin Books (NZ) Ltd, 182–190 Wairau Road, Auckland 10, New Zealand

Penguin Books Ltd, Registered Offices: Harmondsworth, Middlesex, England

First published in Penguin Masterstudies 1985
Revised edition published in Penguin Critical Studies 1990
10 9 8 7

Printed in England by Clays Ltd, St Ives plc
Filmset in Monophoto 9/10 pt Times Roman

Contents

Factors of Significance   7

Plot   12

Stagecraft   21

Speech   32

Parts   53

Tragedy   89

Appendix One: Comparison of *Hamlet* with
some other Elizabethan Revenge Tragedies   103

Appendix Two: Texts   111

Suggestions for Further Reading   117

Factors of Significance

When somebody is telling you a story, if you are going to enjoy it you have to believe what he tells you. If, for example, he begins by telling you that there was once a prince whose father, the king, was everything a man can be, you have to accept his words at their face value. What we are told about the hero's father in *Hamlet* is: ''A was a man, take him for all in all' (I.2.187).

It is not, however, Shakespeare who tells us this. Our informant is the dead king's son. Accordingly we take his words with a pinch of salt, as we would take a similar claim in real life. We consider Hamlet's words in their context. This is the distinguishing feature of drama. Like a Punch-and-Judy man, the dramatist remains invisible and never addresses his audience directly, even when a character as fascinating as Punch or Hamlet is speaking at his command. Even the hero's words must be taken in their context – but, of course, the dramatist has arranged the context too, and he makes it much more significant than any context in real life could be.

What in real life would be an incidental detail can be an important signal on the stage. When, on the occasion of our first encounter with him, Hamlet tells us that, compared with his uncle, his dead father was 'Hyperion to a satyr', we do not merely bear in mind the fact that he may be prejudiced. We store away the details of the contrast, to recall the incident, two acts later, when in an effort to make his mother ashamed of her remarriage Hamlet again compares his father with Hyperion, the god of the sun. We find the coincidence significant. Part of this significance is simply that it recalls the earlier scene, but there is more to it than that. We see more in the comparison of a god with a satyr than we did at first. By now we have become aware of a consistent pattern in which men are compared on the one hand with celestial beings and on the other hand with beasts. A satyr is half man, half beast. And in his reproaches to his mother Hamlet makes further contributions to this pattern. For example, he claims that his father was a being 'Where every god did seem to set his seal' (III.4.62), and describes his uncle as a paddock (toad), a bat, and a gib (tom-cat). The play is not just a re-enactment of an interesting sequence of events. It is also an investigation of the questions prompted by those events, such as, for example, the moral status of humanity.

It is a mistake to read a play as if it were a record of events, taken down as they occurred by a squad of secretaries. As a record, *Hamlet* is completely valueless. The events enacted in it never occurred. What makes *Hamlet* one of the most influential works in world literature is not what happens in it, but what it means. This does not imply that the events in the play – its action – do not matter. It is the action that conveys the meaning. But all those aspects of the action on the stage which Shakespeare has invested with additional significance must also be attended to. It is no use just knowing the story. A comic strip could give you that.

There are five factors of significance in a play – the plot, the stagecraft, the speeches, the various parts to be played, and finally the overall impression to which they all contribute. In this study of *Hamlet* each of these factors is examined in a separate chapter. In order to form a preliminary idea of how they work, however, let us examine a single speech – Gertrude's report of Ophelia's death to Claudius and Laertes in Act IV, Scene 7:

> *There is a willow grows askant the brook,*
> *That shows his hoar leaves in the glassy stream.*
> *Therewith fantastic garlands did she make*
> *Of crowflowers, nettles, daisies, and long purples,*
> *That liberal shepherds give a grosser name,*
> *But our cold maids do dead-men's-fingers call them.*
> *There on the pendent boughs her crownet weeds*
> *Clambering to hang, an envious sliver broke,*
> *When down her weedy trophies and herself*
> *Fell in the weeping brook. Her clothes spread wide,*
> *And mermaid-like awhile they bore her up;*
> *While time she chanted snatches of old tunes,*
> *As one incapable of her own distress,*
> *Or like a creature native and indued*
> *Unto that element. But long it could not be*
> *Till that her garments, heavy with their drink,*
> *Pulled the poor wretch from her melodious lay*
> *To muddy death.*

PLOT. Considered simply as an event, forming part of a causal pattern, the death of Ophelia completes the second of Hamlet's brutalities, thus providing an additional spur to Laertes' revenge.

STAGECRAFT. The elaborate style of this speech marks it off from the talk which has been going on up to this point, and even from Gertrude's words on entering, in which she has already broken the news:

> *One woe doth tread upon another's heel,*
> *So fast they follow. Your sister's drowned, Laertes.*

The effect is to suspend the action on the stage so that the other characters pause, as it were to join the audience in listening. This is an effect which Shakespeare frequently contrives at points where particularly serious attention is called for. He reminds the audience that they are in a theatre in order to focus their attention more directly.

SPEECH: Details which might, superficially, appear to be insignificant reveal themselves to be deeply significant in their context. They contribute specifically to our perception of Ophelia's role in the play, and also generally to our total reception of it.

Ophelia's garlands and her singing recall her mad scenes earlier in this act, but also symbolize the inadequacy of her innocence. The songs she sings are girlish but also knowing. She has chosen weeds for her garlands, a strange combination of freshness and corruption. (We recall that Hamlet warned his mother not to 'spread the compost on the weeds'.) Her fall into the stream is described as if a malign influence was at work in the shape of the willow that caused the accident. Its leaves are 'hoar', it is 'envious', and it grows 'askant'. The alternative name for 'long purples' – 'dead-men's-fingers' – is not brought in for nothing. It contributes to the sinister atmosphere. As it is the name given to the flower by 'cold maids' it also reminds us that Ophelia dies a virgin. It does not, however, suggest that this is cause for rejoicing. She dies cold indeed. Nevertheless the name applied to the flower by 'liberal shepherds' is censured for its grossness, and we recall Hamlet's offensive jokes about 'country matters' at their last meeting, at the play-within-the-play, as well as the bawdy content of some of the songs Ophelia sang in her madness. There is an unresolved ambiguity here.

A similar ambiguity attaches to the way she died. She certainly fell into the brook by accident, but why did she simply lie there until she died? Two incompatible explanations are given: neither is endorsed. The first suggests that she may not have realized her danger, but the second (that she was returning to her element, water), although fanciful, implies that her drowning was voluntary, and thus suicide. Water, like the willow, is emblematic of grief, a point on which Laertes seizes in his lament that follows Gertrude's speech. The brook itself is 'weeping'. The implication is that she died to satisfy her grief.

As regards the connection of the speech with the network of associations which, at this point in the play, has been firmly woven into the text, weeds are a symbol of corrupted nature – Hamlet's 'unweeded garden' – while the mermaid, like the satyr, is half human, half bestial. 'Heavy with their drink' recalls Hamlet's condemnation of the 'swinish' customs of Denmark, making death itself appear as mere bestial oblivion. 'Muddy', it should be noted, is the epithet levelled at himself by Hamlet when he castigates himself for lack of spirit in his third soliloquy.

PARTS. The actors on the stage are distinguished by their differing responses to Ophelia's death. Gertrude's distress is genuine enough. Any kind of unpleasantness causes her anxiety. No sympathy, however, is expressed, and it is relevant to recall that when the mad Ophelia expressed a desire to see her, Gertrude's first reaction was to refuse an interview, a refusal which she only retracted when it was pointed out to her that it would look bad. It is ironical that this speech is spoken by a twice-married adulteress.

The reactions of the listeners are not allowed to interrupt the speech, but are made clear by their subsequent words and behaviour. While doubtless grieved, Laertes makes a spectacle of his grief, self-consciously adding it to his role before storming off the stage. The response of Claudius is entirely hypocritical. Without referring to Ophelia's death he expresses anxiety over Laertes' excited state, declaring that he has been engaged in calming him down, whereas in fact the audience has been watching him incite Laertes.

TRAGEDY. Death is a frequent topic in the play. The speech we are examining builds up to 'death', its final word, and then breaks off, half-way through a line. It leaves us no wiser about death, considered as a topic of discussion; what it does is to convey a feeling that any such discussion is futile. There is no suggestion that death is 'a consummation devoutly to be wished for'. Fearing it, however, seems as pointless as wishing for it. It is waiting for everybody on the stage, as it had been waiting for Ophelia. The word 'muddy' rules out any inference that Ophelia was happy in the water at the last.

The overall impression is one of Ophelia as a passive victim: 'long it could not be . . .'; she was inevitably 'pulled . . . from her melodious lay'. The impression, in short, is one of a catastrophe which is inexplicable and undeserved, but nevertheless in some way fated and appropriate.

Yet because Ophelia either did not recognize her situation or else declined to struggle against it, this effect is not tragic.

It is hardly surprising that an incident in a play cannot be understood in isolation from the rest of the plot. What is surprising is that it should be linked with the rest of the play by other connections which have nothing to do with cause and effect, combining with apparently incidental aspects to produce a total resonance.

Plot

A play is not a report. We read reports for practical purposes, not for their intrinsic interest. If, before he drove off from home to catch the late-night postal collection, the dead man had grumbled: 'It's the last time I'll do this', the traffic police investigating the cause of the accident that befell him on the way would not include this interesting anecdote in their report. If they did include it they would be turning their report into a story. Coincidences only matter in real life if they lead to collisions. They are the products of chance. A coincidence in a story, on the other hand, is an entirely different matter. It is not there by accident. It has been put there to be noticed, because it adds to the story's significance. In a story similarities and oppositions have been arranged beforehand. They are there to be appreciated.

'I'll silence me even here,' Polonius remarks as he hides himself behind the arras at the start of the Closet Scene, and he speaks truer than he knows. He will be dead before he can utter anything more than a cry for help. He is almost anticipating his murderer's obituary rhyme:

> ... this counsellor
> Is now most still, most secret, and most grave,
> Who was in life a foolish prating knave.
> (III.4.214–16)

It is not, however, Hamlet's joke that invests Polonius's words with irony. Irony is not only a matter of words. There is also such a thing as an irony of events, which may remain unspoken and yet which we can still perceive. In this same Closet Scene, for instance, Gertrude has summoned Hamlet to rebuke him, and to instruct him to treat Claudius with more respect. The outcome is that she is herself rebuked, and instructed to treat Claudius with loathing.

Irony is usually a relationship between contradictory utterances linked together – as when St Augustine, praying to be saved from the sins of the flesh, added 'but not yet'. As the 'closet scene' demonstrates, it can also be generated by a relationship between events. A plot is a pattern of events which relates them ironically and in other significant ways, and also has its own overall significance as a whole. Take, for example, the story of the *Three Little Pigs*. Each pig builds a house as a protection against the wolf. In the cases of the pigs who built with straw and with wood, there is an ironic discrepancy between the intention and the result. When their fate is compared with that of the wise little pig who built with brick, however, the story as a whole is found to convey a further meaning to which these sub-plots make their contributions.

Hamlet is constructed in a very similar way. In place of the three pigs threatened by the wolf, we have three young men whose fathers have been killed: Hamlet, Laertes and Fortinbras. Just as two of the pigs employed flimsy building materials and came to grief, so Hamlet and Laertes took the law into their own hands and were themselves killed in the resulting action. Just as the wise pig triumphed by choosing solid material, so Fortinbras triumphs by being obedient to the law. (The fact that this does not make him the hero is the price he has to pay for appearing in a tragedy.)

In these comparable plots, Shakespeare is exploring the implications of one of the popular plot formulas of the Elizabethan stage – the revenge tragedy. Summarized briefly, this plot takes the form of a private vendetta which is providentially converted into a public execution. Its moral is that man proposes but God disposes. It is not an entirely comfortable moral as God works in a mysterious way, and God's ways are not ours. Even in the conventional revenge plot the fate of the revenging hero was pitiful, despite his crimes. Shakespeare's treatment of the plot intensifies this ambiguity.

In the conventional revenge plot the starting-point is a crime which has escaped punishment because it is secret and also because the wrongdoer is beyond the reach of the law. In the case of the Laertes sub-plot, which follows the conventional plot exactly, Hamlet has murdered the revenger's father, but is beyond the reach of the law for reasons which Claudius explains to the revenger in detail at the opening of Act IV, Scene 7.

In seeking revenge the revenger is not looking for justice, which is an impersonal motive. He seeks a personal satisfaction, based on passion. Claudius does not enlist the help of Laertes by telling him that justice, or the general welfare, not to mention the will of heaven, requires Hamlet's death. He reminds him of his love for his father and applauds the criminal unscrupulousness which, in his passion, Laertes boasts of. This development is intrinsic to the conventional revenge plot. The revenger becomes a monomaniac, dares damnation, and sinks to the moral level of his intended victim. (At the time when he murdered Polonius, Hamlet had worked himself into just such a frantic state, in pursuit of his revenge upon Claudius.)

In the conclusion the revenger succeeds. He kills his victim. His success, however, is not his to enjoy. It has only been permitted because it serves the ends of divine justice; that same justice requires the revenger's own death too, because the revenger has usurped the right to condemn to death, which heaven deputes only to its chosen representatives on earth, namely governments. The irony, which remains hidden in revenge tragedy, is that when the government itself is criminal divine justice employs the criminal revenger as its instrument. The implications of this paradox are explored in the case of Hamlet himself. The case of Laertes ends conventionally when, as justice requires, he is killed by the rapier he himself had poisoned.

At the last gasp, Laertes repents. The worthy Fortinbras has nothing to repent of. He, too, has suffered wrongs. He has a slain father, a fall in fortune, and an uncle on his father's throne to contend with. Leading an army of 'lawless resolutes', he at first sets out on the path of revenge. He aims to recover from Denmark certain lands which had belonged to his father, and had been lost to Hamlet's father in fatal single combat. Recalled to obedience by his king, however, he becomes obedient to law instead of trying to take it into his own hands, and is accordingly rewarded.

The main plot steers between these two extremes. At first Hamlet is the conventional revenger – or, at least, does everything he can to change himself into such a figure. His motive is personal satisfaction. It is a ghost that moves him to it, but a ghost is not an angel. Its 'dread command' is not a heavenly one, and indeed its methods of persuasion are very similar to those of Claudius. But by the end of the play the Ghost has ceased to be a force, and is forgotten. The passion for revenge has vanished. Hamlet is conscious only of the requirements of justice, the need to serve as a surgical instrument in the hands of Providence. The same justice which requires the death of Claudius, however, also requires his own. By now he is guilty not only of murder but also of a direct sin against heaven. 'Vengeance is mine; I will repay, saith the lord.' The revenger is guilty of attempting to usurp the divine prerogative.

This blasphemy is demonstrated with unique starkness when Hamlet refrains from killing the praying Claudius because he wishes his victim to suffer the torments of the damned after death. Historical sympathy is required to understand his inaction as a piece of calculated ruthlessness, but that is what it is. A modern audience finds it hard to believe that a man, whose thought they otherwise find fascinating, could believe what Hamlet says at this point. They should remember that Samuel Johnson found Hamlet's projected revenge at this point too horrible to contemplate, and recall the care with which Othello, before murdering Desdemona, offers her time to prepare her soul for death: 'I would not kill thy unprepared spirit.'

A similar effort of historical sympathy is required to perceive that divine justice is a force continuously at work through the plot. It makes acts of personal revenge unnecessary. Providence does not, of course, take the form of miraculous intervention. It manifests itself in events which, superficially considered, are merely natural. But retribution itself is a natural process, when the laws of nature have been broken. When Claudius murdered Hamlet's father he committed regicide and fratricide, and when he married his sister-in-law he committed incest. Just as a wounded body is restless until its wounds are healed, so Nature could not rest until the triple breach in Denmark had been healed. Until he was brought to book, the history of Claudius's reign was bound to be a series of disturbances. When, in answer to Marcellus's suspicion that 'Something is rotten in the state of Denmark', Horatio replies, 'Heaven will direct it', he is not just voicing a pious hope.

The appearance of the Ghost is the first symptom. From then on a tide of events begins to flow against which Claudius struggles vigorously but in vain. He finds his troubles endless. Unforeseeable developments counter every provision he makes, because the causes he tries to manipulate are not natural. They are forced against the natural course of things. The summary of events that Horatio gives to Fortinbras at the end of the play offers an abstract of a typical revenge tragedy:

> So shall you hear
> Of carnal, bloody, and unnatural acts,
> Of accidental judgements, casual slaughters,
> Of deaths put on by cunning and forced cause,
> And, in this upshot, purposes mistook
> Fallen on th'inventors' heads.
>
> (V.2.374–9)

The original crime of Claudius was carnal in its adultery, bloody in its violence, and unnatural on the three counts already mentioned. It therefore precipitated a revolt in Nature which the villain could not control. What appeared to be random events were in fact punishments – 'accidental judgements'. Death was meted out unintentionally – 'casual slaughters'. (Here it is relevant to note Hamlet's comment on the unintentional murder of Polonius: '... heaven has pleas'd it so,/To punish me with this, and this with me' (III.4.174–5).

'Cunning and forced cause' insist that Nature cannot, in the long run, be manipulated to break her own laws. In the end the wrongdoers are caught in their own trap: '. . . purposes mistook,/Fallen on th'inventors' heads'.

Where *Hamlet* departs from the typical revenge formula is that before the catastrophe the hero has ceased to be a revenger, even though he does kill his chosen victim.

Heaven is felt to be behind the course of events in the play. The Providence whose presence Hamlet at last comes to recognize is visible in the endless sequence of accidents, which all point in one direction. There will be no peace in Denmark until the evil has been cleansed. Providence operates on earth like the uneasiness resulting from an illness, which will continue until a cure has been effected:

> *Foul deeds will rise,*
> *Though all the earth o'erwhelm them, to men's eyes.*
>
> (I.2.257–8)

Palliatives will not serve. So Hamlet warns his mother against the application of a 'flattering unction':

> *It will but skin and film the ulcerous place*
> *Whiles rank corruption, mining all within,*
> *Infects unseen.*
>
> (III.4.148–50)

Although his sense of the nature of the illness is mistaken, Claudius makes notable contributions to this sense of the need to get to 'the quick of the ulcer'. He blames himself for being remiss in this respect:

> *We would not understand what was most fit,*
> *But, like the owner of a foul disease,*
> *To keep it from divulging let it feed*
> *Even on the pith of life . . .*
>
> (IV.1.20–23)

The state of Denmark, in which something is rotten, calls for surgery.

'Heaven will direct it' is Horatio's pious answer, but the question remains: who will be the surgeon when the canker that has to be removed is the King and therefore above the law?

It is at this point that *Hamlet* criticizes the convention of revenge by deviating from it. At the end of the typical revenge play divine justice is done by an arrangement in which a set of criminals act as their own executioners, the revenger himself being punished. Thus Hamlet too must be punished for his performance in the revenger's reckless and unscrupulous role. But in the end he does not act like a revenger, he acts as he should have acted at the start, as the only man who could bring Claudius to book, dispassionately, as the instrument of justice, performing his duty as a prince, in public.

Besides inviting a comparison of plots, the play also invites comparison of scenes. The scenes are distinct, complete in themselves, and not directly linked. We rarely find one scene leading into the next. For example, the scene in which Hamlet decides to meet the Ghost is followed not by their meeting but by Laertes' farewell to his family; and after Hamlet's meeting with the Ghost, instead of being shown the effect of their encounter we are presented once again with the family affairs of Polonius.

The most remarkable example of this inconsequential arrangement is the sequence of scenes in the third act – the most intense sequence in the entire play. None of these scenes is linked causally with its predecessor. The second scene – that of the play-within-the-play – has no causal connection with the preceding Nunnery Scene, while the two scenes that follow it were prepared for before it occurred. (Hamlet's summons to an interview with his mother is planned by Polonius at the end of the Nunnery Scene, to which it provides a sequel and a parallel.) Moreover, the first of these two scenes, in which Hamlet spares the life of Claudius and Claudius fails to repent, has no connection with the succeeding Closet Scene.

This marking-off of one scene from another makes it easier to compare them, and thus perceive common patterns. At the time when Shakespeare wrote, the drawing of analogies was a valued intellectual method, in the same way that scientific method is valued now. For example, as society – the 'body politic' – can be compared with a living body made up of parts with different functions, it was argued that society must be governed as a body is: in other words, it must have a head to rule it. It was a familiar habit of thought. As a result, when Claudius in his attempt at prayer laments that his offence has 'the primal eldest curse upon't', an Elizabethan would do more than spot the reference to Cain and Abel. He would also recognize a comparison that extends as far as the detail that Cain's 'offering to the Lord' was rejected, just as Claudius knows his words will not reach heaven.

Despite their lack of causal connection, nearly all the scenes in the first half of the play have a common pattern of mutual interrogation. This pattern is established in the play's opening words:

BARNARDO   *Who's there?*
FRANCISCO   *Nay, answer me. Stand and unfold yourself.*

The situation of two opposing parties, each attempting to unmask the other, is the basic form of dramatic interest until the mousetrap is sprung in the middle of the play.

Comparisons offer themselves right across the play. Jumping from Act I to Act III, an interesting comparison presents itself between Polonius's warning to Ophelia of a threat to her virginity from Hamlet and Hamlet's warning to her in the Nunnery Scene, while the latter can be compared, in this respect, to the way he 'speaks daggers' to Gertrude in the Closet Scene. The comparisons are worth making because they are illuminating. Ophelia is bullied in both scenes, but whereas Polonius is concerned for the effect of her misconduct on his own reputation – 'you'll tender me a fool' – Hamlet is concerned for Ophelia herself and what will become of her. His attack upon his mother is similarly edifying, with the significant difference that he accuses before counselling, as the sin has already been committed.

Another mirroring of one scene in another is that of Act III, Scene 1, in Act V, Scene 1. The earlier scene opens with Hamlet's fourth soliloquy, matched, in the later scene, by his graveyard meditations. His words are interrupted by the entry of Ophelia, apparently at her devotions in the earlier scene, and, in the later, borne as a corpse upon a bier. 'The fair Ophelia!' Hamlet exclaims on each occasion, but the earlier scene ends with his denial of his love for her and the later with his avowal of his love beside her grave.

Nearly every episode has a counterpart. The significance of a passage does not only depend upon its own distinct content and its causal connection with other passages, but also upon its formal differences from other comparable passages. For instance, there is a causal connection between Hamlet's consultation with Horatio before his trap – *The Mousetrap* – is sprung, and the resulting detection of Claudius's guilt. There is, however, a less significant analogy between this consultation and the later one which takes place immediately before Claudius's trap is sprung. It is not merely that the situation is reversed. Hamlet's attitude is reversed as well.

Yet despite these internal correspondences the text is extremely varied. Scenes may be analogous and still vary in tempo or in tone. The first half of the play is composed of a succession of interrogations and investigations. Despite their basic similarity these scenes offer marked contrasts. Compare the difference in tone between the scene in which Hamlet listens to the Ghost and that in which he listens to the Pyrrhus speech, or the difference in tempo between Claudius's welcome to Rosencrantz and Guildenstern and that extended by Hamlet. Contrast the smooth menace of Claudius and the fussy ineptitude of Polonius, both engaged upon the same task. Even within himself Hamlet displays a wide variety of behaviour, ranging from hysterical outburst to dignified courtesy.

The central comparison, however, is that of the main plot of Hamlet's revenge and the Laertes and Fortinbras sub-plots, a comparison which makes the significance of the Hamlet story both explicit, as to the questions it raises, and ambiguous, in the answers it gives. The obvious answer which comparison of the plots alone promotes is the foolish message that it pays to be good. To that, Hamlet might well reply that such a play would be hire and salary, not a tragedy. What tragedy is, and whether *Hamlet* is indeed a tragedy, are questions that cannot be considered until all the factors of significance have been taken into account (see pages 89–102).

When Shakespeare bases the plot of a play on an existing story, our sense of his controlling intention can sometimes be verified by comparing his version with its original. In the case of *King Lear*, for example, the death of Cordelia was inflicted by Shakespeare on his audience, not imposed upon him by the original legend. This fact can be taken to reinforce the less optimistic interpretations of the tragedy.

No such assistance is available in the case of *Hamlet*. The text upon which Shakespeare is presumed to have based his play was a revenge tragedy of Hamlet, famous for its Ghost, known to have been in the possession of his stage company for several years before Shakespeare's tragedy was staged. Although the notion is generally discredited, this earlier version has itself been attributed to Shakespeare. Unfortunately the text of this original is not available for comparison with the existing play; to distinguish it from the latter, this original version is referred to as the *Ur-Hamlet*.

The text upon which the *Ur-Hamlet* was based is, however, available. It is the story of a legendary prince of Denmark named Amleth. This was originally recorded in an eleventh-century chronicle by Saxo Grammaticus, from which it was extracted, with only slight alterations, to be included in a collection of tragic stories by François de Belleforest. Although in the original story Amleth is eventually killed, his death does not feature in the story of his revenge, which he executed without mishap, becoming king of Denmark.

There is no ghost in this original story. Amleth's villainous uncle, who has replaced his brother on the throne after killing him and marrying the widow, is no hypocrite. His crime is not concealed, and he is quick to kill anyone who appears to challenge his position on the throne. To escape this treatment, Amleth feigns madness. Suspecting that he is shamming, his uncle uses agents to sound him out: a beautiful woman, and an old friend of Amleth. Both these characters, however, remain true to Amleth and do not betray him. An attempt to have Amleth put to death in England is foiled in the same manner as in Shakespeare's version, except that there are no pirates to bring Amleth back to Denmark so quickly. He remains in England for a year, but even then contrives to return unexpectedly and slaughter not only his uncle but also most of the court, trapping them under an immense curtain which is then pegged to the ground so that they can be killed at leisure and with impunity. The uncle, however, is killed separately in his private chamber, and, by an ingenious anticipation, with his own sword – as Laertes is killed.

How many of the necessary alterations were effected in the *Ur- Hamlet* and how many were Shakespeare's own can only be conjectured, but two interesting considerations do arise from a comparison of the existing play with the original legend. The feigning of madness to escape suspicion is a conventional tactic of the revenger, but in the case of Hamlet it takes an unusual form. Hamlet does not play the madman, he plays the fool, in the manner of Touchstone in *As You Like It*, using his folly as a stalking-horse to expose the truth. The truth-telling fool is one of Shakespeare's favourite theatrical figures, but he is also a figure of folklore. It is just such a fool that Amleth makes of himself in the original legend. He is not the sophisticated, 'bitter' fool of the tragedy, but he is an all-licensed truth-teller. Nobody takes the truth seriously when a fool speaks it. Thus when Amleth starts sharpening sticks and is asked what he is doing, he replies, apparently daftly, that he is preparing his revenge, and indeed he uses these self-same sticks, when the time comes, to peg down his victims beneath the curtain.

The other consideration relates to the role of Amleth's mother, and the light it throws on the role of Gertrude in Shakespeare's play. The marriage of Gertrude to her brother-in-law is not an invention of Shakespeare, but a feature inherited from the original story. Its presence is not therefore a sign of some unacknowledged obsession of Shakespeare's, such as certain critics have claimed to find in the play. What matters, however, is the question whether the text itself has been distorted by some such obsession. As far as the plot is concerned, it was a common practice for the revenger to become a malcontent, railing satirically against everybody else upon the stage, but especially against the women, and to be disgusted by everything life has to offer and especially by sex.

Stagecraft

The text is like a musical score. It is meant to be performed, and, however well we may know the text, until we envisage it in performance we do not know the play. Although this does not mean that our study of *Hamlet* is incomplete until we have seen it on the stage, it is always revealing to watch a performance in the theatre, no matter how amateur it may be.

To take the most obvious point, when we read a play off the page we read continuously, but this is not what happens upon the stage. On the stage a great deal happens between the lines. Consider the scene (II.2) in which Hamlet welcomes the arrival of his witty friends, Rosencrantz and Guildenstern. He is unreservedly delighted to see them. 'Good lads, how do you both?' A volley of jokes ensues, but then he asks, in all frankness: 'Were you not sent for? Is it your own inclining? Is it a free visitation? Come, come, deal justly with me. Come, come. Nay, speak.' The same question is asked three times, and then is followed by three adjurations.

Repetition on the page appears very differently upon the stage, because on the stage it comes over as a gradual process in which, to his disappointment, Hamlet is gradually forced to realize that his friends' first loyalty is not to him but to his enemy. If Rosencrantz and Guildenstern were hardened deceivers, like Claudius, they would have answered the very first question smoothly with a lie. As it is they remain silent. There is a pause, each time more awkward than the last, after each question and each adjuration, until Guildenstern stammers: 'What should we say, my lord?' When, a few lines later, Guildenstern confesses with sham frankness, 'My lord, we were sent for', it is too late.

These significant pauses are an essential part of a complete reading of the text. It is not, however, necessary to see them on the stage in order to register them. When the play is performed the pauses exist only because the producer has read them into the text. He visualizes them when reading the text because he is visualizing a stage production as he reads. A student of *Hamlet* should read the text in the same way, with an eye perpetually cocked to staging what he reads. He must supply his own stage directions.

The text does include some stage directions, but they are few, although more numerous than at first appears. Some are implicit, as when, in the passage we have just looked at, Hamlet observes in answer to

Guildenstern: 'there is a kind of confession in your looks'. This is a clear direction to the actors playing the parts of false friends. Nevertheless it does not indicate – as a row of dots after each item of Hamlet's speech might indicate – the way in which the words are to be spoken.

Some of the gaps which the producer has to fill are much wider than that one and require more speculation. When the vengeful Laertes bursts in upon the court with his followers, how are the latter to be presented? Like outraged citizens demanding justice, or as the 'rabble' which the messenger deems them to be? And how is Gertrude's attempt to protect her husband to be performed in this scene? How have Hamlet's revelations affected her relations with Claudius? She promised not to betray Hamlet, and we have seen her keep her promise. But that is all we have been shown or are to be shown. Why does she warn the intruders that they are on the wrong scent? In the final scenes Claudius makes several appeals to his wife for sympathy. 'O Gertrude, Gertrude . . .' Is he sharing his sorrows with her, or appealing for support he feels he has lost? Or, to put the question more relevantly, what directions are to be given to the actress playing Gertrude on this (to borrow a phrase from Hamlet's advice to the players) 'necessary question of the play'? No doubt the playwright himself supplied the answer to this question when the play was first put on, but the modern producer must devise an answer for himself, guided by the overall effect which he is aiming at as a result of his reading of the text.

Reading the text therefore involves drawing all sorts of inferences from it. The only kind of inference which belongs to a complete reading of the play is one which requires an answer before it can be staged. Questions which might arise in the mind of a novel-reader – such as how it happened that Claudius, not Hamlet, succeeded to the throne – are irrelevant. It might be argued that the actor playing Hamlet needs to know this, as the answer has a bearing on his relations with Claudius and his court (I.2). This suggestion, however, implies a naturalistic style of acting which is inappropriate to a Shakespearean text. There are plenty of nuances for the actor to register, but these nuances are not symptoms. An actor accustomed to acting Chekhov, confronted with the part of Hamlet, might pick up Gertrude's solicitous remark about Hamlet in the fencing match – that he is 'fat and scant of breath' – and, after due research, incorporate his findings in his performance. In so doing, however, he would only be introducing a distraction. A different style of acting is required. Indeed a different kind of theatre is required. It is not possible to stage an adequate production of *Hamlet* in the kind of theatre Chekhov wrote for.

Naturalistic production, which gives the audience the illusion that they are watching events in real life, was impossible on Shakespeare's stage. To take an obvious example: as performances were given in broad daylight and there was no way of darkening the stage, the inability of the sentries to identify each other immediately in the opening scene of *Hamlet* would contradict the evidence of the spectators' own eyes. One function of their mutual challenge is, quite simply, to establish the fact that the audience is to suppose that the stage is in darkness (although, as we have seen, it also establishes the motif running through the first half of the play).

Even an attempt at naturalistic production would, however, hesitate to shroud the stage in total darkness, and would quickly provide sufficient light to enable the spectators to see the actors distinctly – perhaps even throwing a special light on Horatio. And if an attempt was made to justify this additional illumination realistically by providing one of the late-comers with a lantern, the radiance attached to this source would be outrageously unrealistic. Even in a naturalistic production, the producer's prime consideration will be to direct the audience's attention to significant features of the play.

Once this principle is accepted it is obvious that the lack of naturalism characteristic of Elizabethan stage production was not a handicap. Although unsuitable for Chekhov, the structure of the Elizabethan theatre served to focus the attention of the audience on a play by Shakespeare in the most effective way possible. For this reason modern producers of Shakespeare favour a very similar construction, and it is a theatre essentially similar to Shakespeare's (although equipped with modern lighting) which the student should envisage when considering the staging of a particular scene.

The audience's attention in the theatre is not guided only by what it hears. What it sees upon the stage may contain an additional element of no less significance. For example, there may be a silent character whose very silence is disturbing, like the silence of the Ghost in the opening scene. Or again, the bearing of a speechless character who is only a witness can deeply modify our perception of the scene. In the opening of Act I, Scene 2, the impression of authority conveyed by Claudius's management of the court would be almost conclusive were it not for the sardonic presence of a silent watcher, Hamlet in mourning. Nor need the presence on the stage be human. An object can also convey a comment, especially on the bare Elizabethan stage where objects are so noticeable. Thus in the final scene an essential stage direction calls for the presence in the background of a table, with a goblet placed upon it. The goblet –

the poisoned chalice – provides an ironic comment on the exchange of courtesies between the two contestants in the fencing match.

The way in which one incident mirrors another is often reinforced, quite naturally, by the repetition of a spectacle. The struggle of the soldiers to detain the Ghost upon its first appearance is matched by their struggle to prevent Hamlet from following it upon its second. The stately entrance of the court – including Ophelia – to watch the play-within-the-play is matched in *Hamlet*'s penultimate scene by their furtive entrance to attend a midnight burial, and in the final scene by their entry to watch the fencing match – 'attendants with foils and daggers', to quote the stage direction, 'and all the state'.

Words are not the only significant sounds heard. The contrast between the presence and absence of ceremony in the two scenes last compared is reinforced by the stage direction for trumpets and drums to sound the approach of the court in the later scene. Apart from the sound of trumpets and drums, music plays no part in the presentation of *Hamlet* indicated by the approved texts, although one text, believed to be based on the memories of minor actors, specifies that in her mad scene Ophelia accompanies herself on a lute. Should she play and sing in tune? This question indicates how such details can reinforce the language of the text. 'Sweet bells jangled' was the image which Ophelia herself earlier applied to Hamlet's madness, and we can apply to that lamentation, in retrospect, the frightening observation she makes now: 'Lord, we know what we are, but know not what we may be.'

Noises off-stage also play their part. They are often interruptions, announcing an unexpected arrival, like that of Ophelia herself on her last appearance, or that of Fortinbras and his army at the end of the play. This is not, however, their only function. At the end of Act I, Scene 5, in which Hamlet meets the Ghost, the voice sounding from beneath the stage is part and parcel of the grotesque scene enacted upon it. The salute of guns for Hamlet as his body is borne away at the end of the play (in a second funeral procession) is a significant accompaniment to the action on the stage – matching the discharge of two 'pieces' in the first act, to glorify Claudius's drinking, while Hamlet ponders the loss of honour resulting from one defect of character. Another, more recent, recollection prompted is the use of shots (accompanied by trumpets and drums) to salute Hamlet's first hit in the fatal fencing match, a scene in which Gertrude's pledge to Hamlet's triumph, in the poisoned goblet, also recalls the first occasion when cannon were heard, saluting 'the triumph of his [the King's] pledge'. The noises-off are as close-knit as the episodes in the plot.

None of these sounds operates as a mere 'sound effect'. Their contribution is not to an illusion of 'real life', but to a focusing of attention. The same is true of everything the audience would have seen upon the stage, in addition to its bare boards. The stage properties – the goblet, the skulls, the book Hamlet enters reading – are all intrinsic to the action. A throne might be thrust out on to the stage for the first court scene, and a bed, perhaps, for the Closet Scene, but the stage would be almost always bare. The costumes of the actors, however, provided an additional source of visual significance. This is most obviously true of the royal robes and crown, and the sight of the crown toppling from Claudius's head as he falls in his death agony at the end provides a conclusive symbol of his defeat. Another significant costume detail (again specified in the early version of the text already referred to) is a provision that in the Closet Scene the Ghost should enter in a nightgown – a poignant difference from his previous appearances in full armour. Armour itself, the garb of Fortinbras, contrasting strongly with the gorgeous dress of the courtiers and with Hamlet's black, has a symbolic value. It stands for the readiness to expose 'what is mortal and unsure/To all that fortune, death, and danger dare' – a central issue of the play.

The basic structure of the stage also lends itself to symbolic, rather than realistic, use. Entering by one door and leaving by another, as Fortinbras's army would have to do in Act IV, Scene 4, symbolizes progress. Entering by different doors symbolizes differences between the characters who enter. Thus, in the Mousetrap Scene, Hamlet and Horatio would enter by one door, the court by the other, which they would also use for their hasty exit. Leaving by that door, not by the one he had used to enter, would symbolize Hamlet's pursuit of his revenge.

The stage itself was nearly as big as a tennis court, a large space when only a handful of actors occupied it, unless they were engaged in an extensive action which required them to cover ground – as when, in the first scene, the sentries approach each other, or later, when the group attempts to detain the Ghost. When the only action was speech, in order to concentrate the audience's attention the actors would have to station themselves down-stage, where the platform projected into the audience. To enter or exit at the rear of the stage thus involved covering a considerable distance. Towards the end of the first scene Horatio gives the signal for departure – 'Break we our watch up' – eight lines before the close of it, so that their departure is covered by speech. Very often, however, a departure or arrival – as of the Ghost, for example, or the mad Ophelia, or Hamlet reading a book – is itself a significant spectacle, and no such cover is provided. A striking example is the entry of the court to watch the play. The trumpets and kettledrums sound before they make their appearance, causing Hamlet and Horatio to break off their consultation before the entrance is made – an orderly and ceremonious procession, in marked contrast with the disorder in which they are shortly to leave. A similar provision is made for the entrance of Osrick to inform Hamlet of the duel. 'Peace, who comes here?' says Hamlet, *before* Osrick enters, and the two friends watch with amusement as, before he speaks a word, the actor playing Osrick, now the cynosure of all eyes, makes the most of the opportunity to display by his foppish walk the affectation of the character.

As regards the other features of the stage structure, the two eavesdropping scenes – matching scenes again – require nothing more than a curtain (the arras) hung against the wall space between the two doors at the back (where there may also have been a recess of some sort). The trapdoor is used to serve as a grave, and also as an exit for the Ghost on some but not all occasions. There is a significant difference between those occasions when he leaves of his own volition and those when he is compelled by the approach of day to return to Purgatory; the latter exits must be made underground. There would also be a gallery, at the rear of the stage, but in this play there would appear to be no conclusive need for it.

Because the stage is practically bare of distinctive physical features, and such features as there are can be put to such various uses, unless an additional piece of scenery is placed upon it – such as a throne or a tree – the space provided for acting is absolutely nondescript. Once again, what might at first appraisal appear to be a handicap turns out to be an advantage. When the action is not solidly located in a particular place it can be fluid. The only indication of a shift of scene is the vacation of the stage. Once it has been left empty, when fresh characters appear on it we understand that there has been a removal in space or time or both. Thus, in the first act, when Hamlet follows the Ghost off-stage and then immediately follows it back on again, we understand that they are re-appearing in a different place, although there is not the slightest difference in the appearance of the stage. There is no difficulty in achieving this understanding. A child who had not been warned what to expect would follow it automatically. Nevertheless it is convenient to refer to these departures from the normal course of events as 'conventions' – as if they were agreements made between the audience and the playwright, whereby, to facilitate his presentation, they will overlook impossibilities. Again it is worth pointing out that a child understands this sort of operation without being instructed. When it hears the opening words, 'Once upon a time . . .', it knows at once that impossibilities are to be admitted in the narrative.

In addition to this space convention, Elizabethan plays, thanks to the blankness of the Elizabethan stage, also exploit a time convention. For purposes of the action represented, the time it takes to enact a scene upon the stage may be supposed to have no connection with the time it occupies in the story of the play. The play's opening scene, for instance, is supposed to last from midnight until dawn, whereas upon the stage it only takes some minutes.

The advantage of these conventions is perfectly illustrated in Act II, Scene 2. This is regarded as a single scene only because it never happens in it that the stage is completely empty, although it is actually made up of a series of distinct episodes. It opens with the reception of Rosencrantz and Guildenstern by Claudius and Gertrude, who remain upon the stage when it is over to receive the returned ambassadors to Norway. Polonius, who has ushered in the ambassadors, remains when they have left, to impart his views on Hamlet's distraction. Claudius and Gertrude leave at Hamlet's approach, but Polonius remains, so we are still in the same scene; Hamlet then remains for the arrival of Rosencrantz and Guildenstern, followed by the entry of the players, and the ensuing long scene with them. These episodes can in no way be conceived of as all occurring in the same place or in immediate succession. Considerations of realism are totally ignored, and ignored without loss. The gain is a kaleidoscopic juxtaposition of scenes, more like filmcraft than stagecraft. This montage of episodes facilitates that matching and contrasting of scenes which we have already noted as essential to an appreciation of the plot.

It may be wondered what Hamlet meant in his advice to the players in Act III, Scene 2, when he asserted that the aim of a theatre as conventional as this was 'to hold, as 'twere, the mirror up to nature'. When Renaissance writers used this simile, as they did frequently, the mirror they referred to was a magic one, reflecting the essential truth without its incidental details. All it reflected was the heart of the matter placed before it. This is the gist of Hamlet's advice to the players: they must never distract the attention of the audience from the 'necessary question' at issue in a scene.

A stage which ruled out attempts at naturalism did not handicap but rather assisted a production of that kind. Although they could not distract the audience by cavorting in a realistic setting, the actors could still seduce attention by their gesturing and posturing. 'Nor do not saw the air too much with your hand, thus. But use all gently.' Action must be subordinated to speech.

This prohibition of histrionics does not, however, amount to a plea for naturalism in speech. The verse should be spoken 'trippingly on the tongue'. Following this direction, an actor playing Hamlet would not mutter a comment like 'A little more than kin and less than kind', however psychologically convincing such a rendering might seem. He would speak out clearly so that the audience could hear, placing emphasis to bring out the meaning, not to indicate the state of mind of a fictitious speaker. Not that the words were to be proclaimed like a public announcement – 'I had as lief the town crier spoke my lines.' But the variations in tone and speed, the pauses, changes in volume and intensity, and the articulation would be plainly artificial and beyond the represented character. To quote Hamlet yet again, the duty of an actor speaking Shakespeare's verse is to bring out its 'form and pressure'.

The foundation of an Elizabethan play was speech. At times the action required the actors to fight, fence, march, walk in procession, dig, hide or disappear – performances which could be executed convincingly on a bare stage because the only properties, if any, which they required were such as the actor himself carried in his hand. For the rest, all they could do on that bare stage was to speak to themselves and to one another, but that was enough. Speech is a form of action. In the first two scenes the characters use words to challenge, welcome, instruct, command, reprimand, implore, announce, consent, refuse and confide. There is nothing unnatural about such activities, but it is unnatural to concentrate so absolutely on verbal performance to the practical exclusion of all else – and when one is silent oneself, to do little more than show that one is listening to someone else who holds the stage at that particular moment.

Normally the proper situation on the stage for a Shakespearian actor is the place that will reinforce his words if he is speaking, or, if he is silent, will direct attention to whoever is speaking – except when, as in the case of Hamlet in the first scene at court, the actor's silence is itself a message. In that scene Hamlet must be standing where his silence will be noticed. The centre of attention is the middle of the front of the stage, where the Elizabethan actor had the audience all around him. This downstage position makes soliloquies intimate. It is no less advantageous when two characters are engaged in verbal thrust and parry. And when the stage is crowded, this centre of attention is even more important. The actors group themselves accordingly around it. In the final scene, for example, it is the spot where Hamlet dies, and where Fortinbras, striding in to stand by the body, then visibly takes his place – even down to the detail of having Horatio at hand.

Significant groupings, such as this of Hamlet, Fortinbras and Horatio, would retain their value even if the actors were as motionless as statues. In the scene in which Ophelia distributes flowers, for example, the recipients – Claudius, Gertrude and Laertes – will not contribute to the effect if they register strong feelings. They will simply distract attention from Ophelia. They are sufficiently distinguished by the flowers she selects for each of them, provided they are standing well away from each other so that she has to move some distance from one to another.

On the Elizabethan stage the actors are not simulating natural behaviour. They are on display, as the audience cannot fail to notice. Playing to the audience is the hallmark of the actor's style. On any stage the actor must, of course, be aware of his audience, but on the Elizabethan stage he must show the audience this awareness. When he speaks, for example, it must be clear that, although he is addressing other characters upon the stage, his speech is ultimately directed to listeners who are off it. No effort is made to diminish the audience's awareness of its own actual location, and that of the action it is watching: in a theatre. On the contrary, Shakespeare often goes out of his way to remind the audience of this reality at those very moments when the intensity of the action on the stage might, in spite of all the palpable pretence of theatre, induce the audience to forget it.

In *Julius Caesar*, for instance, when Caesar has just been assassinated and his murderers are bathing their hands in his blood, one of them says:

> *How many ages hence*
> *Shall this our lofty scene be acted over*
> *In states unborn and accents yet unknown!*

The effect is to remind the audience that they are not present at the scene enacted before them, but at one of those future representations which are being anticipated in the speech they are listening to. In *Coriolanus*, at the moment when the hero makes his fatal decision, he too returns the audience's attention to the theatre (in which the roofing over the stage was known as 'the heaven'):

> *Behold the heavens do ope,*
> *The gods look down, and this unnatural scene*
> *They laugh at.*

Similarly, in the final scene of *Hamlet*, the dying prince addresses the other characters on the stage as actors with walk-on parts, dismissing them to join the audience:

> *You that look pale and tremble at this chance,*
> *That are but mutes or audience to this act . . .*
>   (V.2.328–9)

This device destroys any illusion the audience may have been enjoying that they were watching a reality. It *recalls* them to reality. If they lose interest in the action on the stage as a result, the move is disastrous. If they still concentrate upon the play, however, though realizing that a play is all it is, their attention becomes responsible because it is voluntary. They are not being beguiled by the actors, but joining them to consider what it means to be summoned by fate. Coriolanus compares himself to a 'dull actor' who fluffs his lines, and, in his final despair, Macbeth speaks of

> *A poor player*
> *That struts and frets his hour upon the stage*
> *And then is heard no more.*

Spoken by an apparent king, this is a striking reminder of actuality. This same effect is even stronger in Hamlet's third soliloquy, when he compares his own performance with that of the player he has just been listening to.

References to the theatre are common throughout Shakespeare's work, but nowhere else do they appear as frequently as in *Hamlet*. The audience is not only often reminded that it is in a theatre; theatrical concepts are explored in the dialogue. We cannot know whether the play-within-the-play was already a feature of the *Ur-Hamlet* plot. A play-within-the-play supplies the climax in Kyd's *Spanish Tragedy*, which launched the genre upon the Elizabethan stage, but in that case the actors who take part in the inner play are masquerading characters from the play itself. In *Hamlet* Shakespeare brings actors into the action at this point, so that we have the spectacle of actors on the stage before us who are acting the part of actors acting on another one. Whether or not he inherited this feature, he makes full use of it to keep the idea of theatre in view, not merely by allusion but by direct representation, as also happens in the Pyrrhus recitation and in the two discussions of theatrical matters. The effect exceeds alienation. The stage becomes a central image of the play.

Even when the action has no connection with theatre, characters discuss it in theatrical terms, as when Hamlet describes his impromptu measures against Rosencrantz and Guildenstern by saying that his brain had begun to act before he had time for a prologue. Suspicion of the Ghost is expressed by saying that he may have put on King Hamlet's theatrical get-up, or 'shape', a term used all through the play in the discussion of genuineness or style. 'Show', another word with theatrical connections, is used in the same way. The theatre thus provides a constant frame of reference. In the opening scene, Horatio addresses the Ghost as a figure in a masquerade:

> *What art thou that usurpest this time of night,*
> *Together with that fair and warlike form*
> *In which the majesty of buried Denmark*
> *Did sometimes march?*

(I.1.46–9)

The Ghost is wearing the dead king's costume. In the final scene, Hamlet is carried to a stage in the *likeness* of a soldier.

A stage effect that reinforces this feature of the text is the frequent use of a stage situation involving some of the characters upon it in the role of spectators, watching the behaviour of other characters – the effect of a play-within-the-play. Thus, in the opening scene, an audience gathers on the stage to watch the Ghost. At the end an audience gathers to watch a fencing match. Twice, characters watch Hamlet from behind a curtain. Horatio provides an audience for Hamlet's mockery of Osrick. Half-way through the Gravedigger's clowning, Horatio and Hamlet slip on to the stage to share in the audience's enjoyment of it.

Speech

Blank verse, like other conventional features, was accepted on the Elizabethan stage as natural. It is not the only form of speech to be heard in *Hamlet*. To take the most obvious exception first, the play-within-the-play is couched in couplets; this marks it off from the other action on the stage. Couplets are also used in the course of dialogue, to point an aphorism, as when Ophelia tells Hamlet:

> *. . . to the noble mind*
> *Rich gifts wax poor when givers prove unkind.*
> (III.1.100–101)

They are also used, sometimes but not invariably, to mark the end of a scene:

> *The play's the thing*
> *Wherein I'll catch the conscience of the King.*
> (II.2.602–3)

Or they may serve both purposes at once, as in:

> *Foul deeds will rise,*
> *Though all the earth o'erwhelm them, to men's eyes.*
> (I.2.257–8)

The blank verse itself is not all of a piece. In particular, the verse of the Pyrrhus speech, recited first by Hamlet and then by the player, is more thickly decorated with figures of speech and startling images than the verse spoken by the characters at large in the play:

> *. . . roasted in wrath and fire,*
> *And thus o'er-sizèd with coagulate gore,*
> *With eyes like carbuncles, the hellish Pyrrhus*
> *Old grandsire Priam seeks.*
> (II.2.460–62)

But to use the distinction employed by Gertrude when she requests Polonius (II.2.95) to get on with what he has to say, even this is not a case of art flourishing at the expense of matter. The alliteration of the first line connects anger with anguish. The 'conceit' in the next line – suggesting that Pyrrhus is coated so thickly with the blood of his victims that he looks bigger than he is – emphasizes the monstrosity of the slaughter. The image of the carbuncle connects the redness of the killer's eyes with the hardness of a stone. Thus what appears to be mere decoration of plain meaning in fact adds to the plain meaning.

This is true of every deviation from plain speech in the play. Characters rarely speak as plainly as the gravedigger does – though even he plays with words. But their deviation from plain speech is always significant. Language supplements the action. This is most obvious when it describes events – which may not occur on the stage, as when Gertrude describes the death of Ophelia. Description is also used, however, to guide our attention to what is actually happening; for instance, the first appearance of the Ghost is commented upon by the actors as it occurs. Afterwards, they describe its appearance twice, to remind us of its majesty and terror. This can be done by characters who have not even witnessed the scene of which their speech reminds us. On the Ghost's appearance in the Closet Scene, Gertrude tells Hamlet:

> *Forth at your eyes your spirits wildly peep,*
> *And, as the sleeping soldiers in th'alarm,*
> *Your bedded hair like life in excrements*
> *Start up and stand on end.*
>
> (III.4.120–23)

At first this description – guiding our perception of Hamlet's behaviour on the stage before us – might seem to be obscured by this comparison with a guard standing to, in the middle of the night, but it serves to remind us of the first appearance of the Ghost to the soldiers on watch at midnight. The idea of life moving the hair, which is an immobile excrescence of the body, similarly indicates the horror of a ghost, especially when we remember that hair continues to grow on a recent corpse.

In this way what might at first appear to be pointless decoration serves to knit the play together – in this case, two matching scenes. Similar service is rendered by the use of allied images ('image patterns') to keep the underlying meaning of the action on the stage in view as it occurs. We have seen that an essential feature of the plot is the operation of Divine Justice, which will not leave Denmark in peace until the wrong of Claudius's crime has been put right. A sense of this operation is conveyed throughout the play by references to a sickness, in particular an ulcer, which calls for radical treatment, and will not let the body rest until it is cured. We have also noted how the notion of 'show' is intrinsic to a complete perception of the action. Images of concealment and pretence are also continually employed to convey this idea:

> *Mother, for love of grace,*
> *Lay not that flattering unction to your soul,*
> *That not your trespass but my madness speaks.*
> (III.4.145–7)

In addition to the reference to grace, which is associated with Divine Justice, we have here the reference to a disease which no soothing ointment will cure, although it may give the appearance (show) of doing so.

Images from one scene, repeated in another, also serve to establish significant connections. In Act IV, Hamlet does not only attempt to 'catch the conscience of the King'; he attempts to catch the Queen's conscience as well. The image of a mirror which reflects the truth is employed in connection with both operations – the play, which Hamlet tells the players should present such an image, and the mirror which he warns his mother he is going to show her – 'Where you may see the inmost part of you'.

This is the scene where Hamlet claims that he is 'cruel only to be kind', a phrase recalling his first line in the play – 'A little more than kin, and less than kind' – defining his changed family relationships. There are many such echoes. Particularly ironic is that when Claudius, invoking the sanctity of kingship to protect himself against the invaders of his palace, declares, like Hamlet, 'There's a divinity . . .'

More continuous than these echoes is the frequent repetition of key words ('iterative words') which remind the audience of the central issues. We have already noted 'shape' and 'show'. What makes these words particularly valuable is their ambiguity. Each can be used to denote an unreliable appearance and also an appearance which is a reliable sign. 'Show' is used in both senses. In the second scene of the play, when Hamlet tells his mother that he has 'that within which passes show' he means by 'show' an outward 'trapping'. When Claudius says that Hamlet's persistent mourning 'shows a will most incorrect to heaven' he means that it is a sure sign of this defect. 'Conscience', another iterative word, is similarly ambiguous. It can mean a judge of right and wrong, as when Hamlet, talking to Horatio just before the fencing match, points out that it is now 'perfect conscience' for him to kill Claudius; or it can mean the reflective self-examination which 'makes cowards of us all'.

Ambiguity of this kind, especially in the shape of the pun, is a characteristic device of Shakespeare, and at one time was regarded as frivolous. More recently it has been recognized as a means of fusing ideas. The fact that in surprising us it also amuses us does not mean that a pun cannot be taken seriously. Wit is not incompatible with seriousness, witness the example of Hamlet himself. The words with which he at last dispatches Claudius feature a pun:

> *Is thy union here?*
> *Follow my mother.*
> (V.2.320–21)

The pun fuses the treachery of the poisoned pearl ('union') with Claudius's marriage (union) with his sister-in-law. Hamlet has an eye for such connections. He even puns at the solemn moment when he first sees the Ghost:

> *Thou comest in such a questionable shape . . .*
> (I.4.43)

Both 'questionable' and 'shape' are punned on here. The form of the ghost invites investigation: what does it want? But it is also a suspect masquerade. A moment later Hamlet gives further proof that he can be witty in earnest, when he warns his companions who try to detain him: 'By heaven, I'll make a ghost of him that lets me!'

Ambiguity is found in the speech of other characters, but apart from Polonius – who, when it comes to language, might be called his feeble opposite – Hamlet is the only one who puns deliberately and consistently. He is also the only character whose style of speech reveals the actual working of his mind. The language of the others reveals only their overt intentions, but we can watch Hamlet thinking as he speaks. His habit of mind is nowhere more evident than in his consciousness of ambiguity, in his prose no less than in his verse. He adopts prose, along with his 'antic disposition', to trick his enemies.

For this reason there is an unusually high proportion of prose in *Hamlet*, compared with other tragedies. The reason is that on the Elizabethan stage a noble character uses prose when talking to other noble characters only when they are entertaining one another with witty conversation. Otherwise a noble character will use prose when he condescends to converse with menial characters, mostly (as when Hamlet talks to the Gravedigger) for entertainment. If he goes mad, or pretends to do so, he will also speak in prose. When Hamlet appears to be demented, Claudius and his courtiers speak in prose to humour him. It might be said that Hamlet adopts his 'antic disposition', together with prose speech, in order to be able to talk to them. He cannot address them in blank verse as people he respects.

At the end of the scene in which we first see him, in the presence of Claudius and his court, the only person he can bring himself to address directly is his mother. His other remarks are purely throwaway observations, addressed to nobody in particular – almost asides to the audience. 'But break, my heart, for I must hold my tongue,' he says, after the rest have gone. Although he cannot talk to courtiers, he nevertheless speaks freely with soldiers and scholars, as he demonstrates immediately afterwards when Horatio and the others come in to tell him what they have seen. With them he uses blank verse, and continues to do so, even after he has begun to play the fool and speak in prose at court.

It is interesting to note the shifts from prose to verse and back again in Act III. In the first scene Hamlet soliloquizes in blank verse, but shifts to prose to speak to Ophelia; she begins in verse, shifting to prose only after his abrupt question, 'Ha, ha! Are you honest?', suggests that he is demented. The next scene opens with Hamlet talking to the players. He does so in prose, not to fool them but because he is condescending to their lowly status. He also uses prose to converse with Polonius, Rosencrantz and Guildenstern, but, alone with Horatio, adopts verse. 'I must be idle,' he reminds Horatio when the court arrives to watch the play, and immediately switches back to prose. They return the compliment in their remarks to him. After the hasty departure of the court he is beside himself with success, and now converses in prose even when he and Horatio are alone together. In the Closet Scene he honours his mother by using verse.

The prose in which Hamlet displays his quality of mind is not used because it is socially appropriate, as it is when he converses with the players, but as a sign of disrespect:

KING *Now, Hamlet, where's Polonius?*
HAMLET *At supper.*
KING *At supper? Where?*
HAMLET *Not where he eats, but where 'a is eaten.*

He has forced his enemy into the role of straight man in a comic turn. This is what Shakespeare's fools try to do with everyone they meet, although sometimes they get a taste of their own medicine in reply. The basis of Hamlet's fooling is his mastery of ambiguities. His victim finds himself perpetually at cross purposes. Claudius took Hamlet's words to mean what they would be most likely to mean, only to find that they meant something else. The trick can, however, also be played in reverse:

POLONIUS *What is the matter, my lord?*
HAMLET *Between who?*

A similar trick is to use a quick eye for logical connections to produce bizarre illustrations of simple ideas. This has the effect of a riddle. 'For you yourself, sir, shall grow old as I am – if, like a crab, you could go backward,' Hamlet promises Polonius. The effect is lunatic, but, as Polonius observes, 'there is method in't'. There is even a logical connection in the genuine article, as produced by Ophelia in her madness: 'They say the owl was a baker's daughter. Lord, we know what we are, but know not what we may be.' (Like Ophelia herself when she was happy, the baker's daughter could not foresee what she would become.)

From the end of Act IV, when Hamlet returns to Denmark after escaping from the pirates, there is no more of this fooling – although Hamlet receives some of the same treatment from the Gravedigger. Now that his mind is clear, he is free to speak to the court in his own person, and he does so in verse. This has an interesting effect on his private conversations with Horatio. When he spoke to the court in prose, he addressed Horatio in verse as a mark of their special relationship. Now that he speaks to the court in verse, he uses prose with Horatio – of an easy, clear, but by no means casually constructed kind. (As we mentioned earlier, in so far as it was the medium of repartee prose was in any case appropriate at court in its proper place – witness the case of Osrick, and also the witty opening skirmish with Rosencrantz and Guildenstern before Hamlet suspects them.)

The use of ambiguity in Hamlet's fooling is premeditated. He lays verbal traps for his enemies. Puns like 'questionable shape', on the other hand, have the effect of coming to him in the course of speaking. The verse in which they appear is not rhetorical; it does not seem to be following a plan, but rather to be following the movements of his mind as he thinks. Ambiguities are like switch-points. This applies to ambiguous images, no less than to ambiguous words. 'To die, to sleep . . .' The image has been chosen as an image of rest, and that is how he considers it for four lines, but dwelling on the image uncovers an ambiguity which switches him on to a different line of thought: 'To sleep – perchance to dream' (III.1.64–5). He recoils at the thought of 'what dreams may come', and his thoughts have taken him to a goal at which they were not originally aimed. His soliloquy does not expound an idea he has already had: it is a flow of thought. He is thinking *as* he speaks, not *before* he speaks. He becomes aware of the full implications of what he has said only after he has said it. The effect of improvisation is the opposite of that of rhetoric. In rhetorical speech the resources of language are all efficiently marshalled to produce a calculated effect. Hamlet's speech is distinguished by its extempore quality from that of the other characters and brings him closer to the audience, who can see him from the inside while they can only see the others from the outside.

Even when Hamlet does employ rhetoric, until Act IV his style distinguishes him from the other characters by revealing more of the speaker's mind. His rhetoric is less public, more private, than theirs, more peculiar to him. This does not mean that it is impossible to address somebody rhetorically in private; the art of persuasion is not confined to public meetings, and the art of persuasion is what rhetoric is. The point is that the art of persuasion has nothing to do with self-expression, but as long as he remains undecided Hamlet cannot help expressing himself.

Take, as an example of this extra depth, the following passage from the series of speeches directed at his mother, to make her repent her marriage:

> *That monster custom, who all sense doth eat,*
> *Of habits devil, is angel yet in this,*
> *That to the use of actions fair and good*
> *He likewise gives a frock or livery*
> *That aptly is put on.*

> (III.4.162–6)

This may be paraphrased as follows. 'You can get used to anything. This can be a bad thing; when you get used to evil-doing your conscience is dulled. On the other hand, if you persist in doing what is right it will become a habit, so that eventually it calls for little effort.' Compare this with the following passage from the speech in which Rosencrantz reassures Claudius that it is his duty, as a king, to take the fullest precautions to ensure his own security. Having already produced one image of a monarch's downfall, which likens its effect on lesser mortals to that of a whirlpool, he adds a second comparison:

> *. . . or 'tis a massy wheel*
> *Fixed on the summit of the highest mount,*
> *To whose huge spokes ten thousand lesser things*
> *Are mortised and adjoined; which when it falls,*
> *Each small annexment, petty consequence,*
> *Attends the boisterous ruin.*

(III.3.17–22)

This may be paraphrased as follows. 'The downfall of a king involves the ruin of the many lesser beings whose fortunes depend on his.'

As comparison of the two paraphrases indicates, Rosencrantz takes six lines to convey only half as much information as is contained in Hamlet's five lines – and in any case the message only repeats that conveyed in his previous comparison. This does not mean, however, that Hamlet's use of language is in some way superior. Considered as an attempt to persuade, Hamlet's sentence is over-packed. It is a principle alike of rhetoric as of modern communication theory – the principle of 'redundancy' – that it is as well to say the same thing at least twice. Hamlet does not say the same thing twice even when he appears to do so. 'Fair and good' attributes two different qualities to the actions it commends. 'Fair' suggests not 'right' but 'fine'. The actions are noble as well as good. Similarly 'frock or livery' is a revision. Livery is not the property of the person who wears it. There are clearly additional meanings implicit in Hamlet's words which have not been included in our paraphrase. Where items in Rosencrantz's lines are linked, they merely repeat one another. 'Adjoined' adds nothing to 'mortised'. 'Small annexment' and 'petty consequence' merely repeat 'lesser things . . . mortised and adjoined'. ('Consequence' here means something which follows along, not 'result'.) The paraphrase renders Rosencrantz's message in its entirety. His meaning is explicit. Much of Hamlet's meaning is implicit.

Moreover, Rosencrantz's image is readily grasped. It is in any case an adaptation of a stock image of the period – Fortune's Wheel, which we have already seen bowled downhill in the course of the Pyrrhus speech (II.2.493–4). Stock imagery naturally lends itself to the expression of truisms, such as that which Rosencrantz is pronouncing here, or to commonplace sentiments, as when in Act I, Scene 2, declaring his readiness to grant Laertes his wish, Claudius assures him:

> *The head is not more native to the heart,*
> *The hand more instrumental to the mouth,*
> *Than is the throne of Denmark to thy father.*
>
> (I.2.47–9)

Even if it were not a stock image, it would be easily visualized because it is not merely alluded to. Four lines are devoted to describing it, and its attachments, before it is set in motion. It serves as a clear diagram and no ambiguity is involved in it.

Hamlet's image of custom as a monster differs from this unambiguous diagram in every respect. It is not a stock image. Indeed, it is a startling comparison. Custom, after all, is 'second nature' to us. But this is exactly what Hamlet is denying: custom is *not* true nature. It distorts our true nature. The introduction of a monster is therefore an assistance to our understanding. It is not, however, explicit; we have to think about the image in order to grasp its meaning. No attempt is made to describe it, as Rosencrantz describes his wheel. Nor is it easy to visualize a monster that devours an awareness ('sense'), and sometimes, in the 'shape' of an angel, hands out clothing. The move from 'habits' to clothing is one of those switches caused by the ambiguity of a word. 'Habit' can mean either 'custom' or 'clothing'. Here again the ambiguity is significant. By linking 'custom' with 'clothing' the double meaning emphasizes that nothing that is customary is natural. Its effect is only external. (Once again, we are reminded of one of the central issues of the play.) The ambiguity even invests the whole tenor of Hamlet's advice to Gertrude with irony. He is advising her to trust herself to a monster, so that she may 'assume a virtue' which is not truly hers.

His thought is not original, but it is not commonplace. Nevertheless his choice of images is commonplace. Eating and putting on clothes are everyday activities. It is characteristic of his forms of speech to employ such homely imagery to express ideas which are never trite and are sometimes startling:

> *O God, I could be bounded in a nutshell and count myself a king of infinite*
> *space, were it not that I have bad dreams.*

> (II.2.253–5)

A similar modesty is also found in his diction. He chooses simple words on most occasions. Compare his vocabulary here with that of Rosencrantz who, in the interests of dignity, uses 'high diction'. 'Summit' instead of 'top'; 'mortised and adjoined' instead of 'fixed'; 'consequence' instead of 'connection'.

Hamlet's speech is rhetorical in the sense that it is aimed to have a calculated effect upon the listener, but it is more attuned to the speaker's mind than to the listener's. This shows in its complexity and compression, its disregard of norms, the comparative absence of set forms. This neglect of set forms is also a quality of his versification. The iambic pentameter, like all other metres, is a set pattern of feet. In this case each foot is what is called an 'iamb'. An iamb is composed of two syllables, of which the first is unstressed and the second stressed. Thus you pronounce the word 'absent' as an iamb when you ask, 'Why did he ab*sent* himself?', but not when you ask, 'Why did he go *ab*sent?' There are five iambs in an iambic pentameter, as:

> Ab*sent* | thee *from* | fe*li* | ci*ty* | a*while*.

It is an excellent metre to use in a play because it approximates reasonably closely to the rhythm of natural speech, and it can be stretched without snapping.

In *Hamlet* the iambic pentameter is subjected to a lot of stretching. More than one eighth of its lines have not ten syllables (which is all that five iambs amount to) but eleven. The additional syllable, however, is usually unstressed, tacked on to the end after the iambic pentameter has been completed:

> To *be* | or *not* | to *be* | that *is* | the *quest* | (ion)

When it appears in that position, although it is in excess of the requirements of the metre ('hypermetric'), the irregularity does not force itself on the attention of the listener. If anything, the line sounds smoother and more conversational – less formal only in the sense of being casual. The case is very different, however, when a line that contains an excess syllable ends with a stressed syllable. Hamlet's third soliloquy, whose opening line is quoted above, opens with four eleven-syllable lines, all ending with unstressed syllables:

> *To be, or not to be – that is the question;*
> *Whether 'tis nobler in the mind to suffer*
> *The slings and arrows of outrageous fortune*
> *Or to take arms against a sea of troubles . . .*
>
> (III.1.56–9)

It reads easily. The case is very different with the fifth line:

> *And by opposing end them. To die, to sleep –*

This line too contains an extra syllable, but this time the line ends with an iamb. When the extra syllable is tacked on to the line after the iambic pentameter has been completed it is ignored. But in this case it has to be fitted somewhere into the iambic pentameter. What happens in this case is that the line has to stop and start again.

> And *by* | oppos | ing *end* (them). |
> 　　　　　　　　　　　　To *die,* | to *sleep*

This heavy break is meaningful. Hamlet is beginning a new line of thought when he says, 'To die ...' A similar intrusion of an extra syllable occurs in the lines spoken to Gertrude which have just been discussed.

> *Of habits devil, is angel yet in this*

Here the hypermetric syllable is squeezed in, so that 'devil' is pronounced as one syllable, or at least counts as only one. The result is a sense of pressure and hurry, which is also dramatically appropriate. Even greater disturbance may be introduced into the verse, as in the following:

> *I should ha' fatted all the region kites*
> *With this slave's offal. Bloody, bawdy villain!*
> 　　　　　　　　(II.2.576–7)

The first of these two lines is a regular iambic pentameter. The next has an excess syllable, as in the cases we have just examined. Although the last syllable is unstressed, it cannot, however, be read like

> *To be, or not to be – that is the question;*

Both lines have a break in the middle, but the break is far more pronounced in

> *With this slave's offal. Bloody, bawdy villain!*

The word 'offal' (with its slaughterhouse associations) has to be swallowed up in a single syllable. The effect is that the second half of the line develops a rhythm which is the opposite of the iambic. Instead of a pattern of unstressed syllables followed by stressed, we have stressed syllables followed by unstressed, a thumping ('trochaic') metre:

> *bloody,* | *bawdy* | *villain!*

The same reversal occurs in the next line. This time the syllable treated as excess is the first one, and we get

Re | *morse*less, | *treach*erous, | *leche*rous, | *kind*less | *vill*ain.

The galloping, thumping rhythm conveys a sense of runaway violence which is entirely appropriate.

Superficially considered, Polonius sometimes resembles Hamlet in his speech – when he plays with words, for example. He aspires to wit. When Ophelia mentions Hamlet's 'tenders of his affection', he picks up the word 'tender':

> *Tender yourself more dearly,*
> *Or – not to crack the wind of the poor phrase,*
> *Running it thus – you'll tender me a fool.*
> (I.3.107–9)

But Hamlet does not advertise his verbal skills like that, nor is he so explicit. Like Hamlet, Polonius also monitors his own speech – deprecating the elaboration of his own rhetorical figure when imparting his view of the cause of Hamlet's madness to Claudius and Gertrude:

> *That he's mad, 'tis true. 'Tis true, 'tis pity,*
> *And pity 'tis 'tis true – a foolish figure.*
> (II.2.97–8)

But Hamlet monitors his own speech to catch the implications of what he has said, not to find out how it sounds to an audience.

There is a closer resemblance to Hamlet's use of language in some of Claudius's speeches. Claudius is another victim of conscience:

> *. . . like to a man to double business bound*
> *I stand in pause where I shall first begin,*
> *And both neglect.*
> (III.3.41–3)

No image of Hamlet's is more powerful or full of meaning than Claudius's expression of the terror of divine judgement, which compels the wrongdoer to give evidence against himself, 'Even to the teeth and forehead of our faults' (III.3.63). The agony of the image is felt directly, before it is elucidated. It would seem to mean that no face can be put upon sin.

There are similar passages in his seduction of Laertes. No image in the play is more homely than the comparison with a burning candle which illustrates his observation that love extinguishes itself by its own process. The 'spendthrift sigh,/That hurts by easing' has all the compression and self-contradiction of Hamlet's complex utterances. But these are lapses from his normal standard of rhetoric. He does not use language to explore himself. When we listen to him on the stage he is generally using it to control the actions of the other characters on it, so his words are addressed entirely to them, not to himself. This may make his discourse less interesting than that of Hamlet. It is, however, most important to realize that rhetoric is not necessarily vicious. The rhetorician has to think before he speaks, but it is not only crimes that are premeditated. He may not choose to reveal himself, but self-revelation is not the main function of language. Nor is it the case that, because it is deliberate, rhetoric has to be empty and insincere.

Rhetoric is the technique of verbal communication. In Elizabethan times verbal activity was a field of public entertainment, to be enjoyed in sermons, pamphlets, the law courts and in courtly society, as well as in the theatre. This means that the theatre audience was well informed. Just as spectators at Wimbledon can recognize and judge a passing shot, a large section of the audience for which Shakespeare wrote could recognize and appreciate a metaphor. This was particularly true of the lawyers and courtiers in the audience, but as the study of rhetoric was placed at the centre of the curriculum in grammar schools the connoisseurs included people who had little practical use for rhetoric in their daily lives.

Lawyers prized a skill which enabled a speaker to continue with a clear line of thought – the 'argument' – throughout a speech, keeping it firmly in his listeners' minds from beginning to end. Not so much concerned with presenting a case as with self-presentation, the courtier – of whom Osrick is a satirical caricature – is more interested in the 'ornaments of speech' by means of which, by intriguing his listener, the rhetorician aimed at winning his attention. There are two sorts of ornament. One is the 'scheme' – in other words, giving a sentence a pattern over and above the arrangement required by grammatical construction. For example:

> *What to ourselves in passion we propose,*
> *The passion ending, doth the purpose lose.*
> (III.2.204–5)

In addition to the arrangement required by the grammar and by the couplet form, the words in this sentence are arranged in a scheme, 'antithesis', in which opposites are balanced against each other. 'To ourselves' (as in keeping something 'to ourselves') is the opposite of 'lose', so that the beginning of the sentence is opposed to its conclusion. 'In passion' balances 'the passion ending', and 'propose' is opposed to 'purpose', which almost repeats it. Another example of a scheme, less tightly structured but still more formal than common speech, is Hamlet's reply to his mother's question why bereavement seems so 'particular' with him:

> *'Tis not alone my inky cloak, good mother,*
> *Nor customary suits of solemn black,*
> *Nor windy suspiration of forced breath . . .*
> (I.2.77–9)

Polonius's introduction to his production of Ophelia's letter is full of examples, and is ridiculous. However, it is not ridiculous because it employs various schemes, but because it does so to no purpose. Compare the way in which a scheme is used by Hamlet to explain his final view of death:

> *If it be now, 'tis not to come. If it be not to come, it will be now.*
> *If it be not now, yet it will come.*
>
> (V.2.214–16)

The trope, the other sort of ornament, is a use of language which is not intended to be taken literally, as in metaphor, irony, or hyperbole. Hamlet mocks Laertes' use of hyperbole at Ophelia's grave, when he extravagantly orders the gravediggers to pile the earth in upon him, 'Till of this flat a mountain you have made'.

Hyperbole is a favourite trope of Laertes in his role as revenger:

> *I dare damnation. To this point I stand,*
> *That both the worlds I give to negligence,*
> *Let come what comes, only I'll be revenged . . .*
> (IV.5.135–7)

In this case, however, hyperbole is not ridiculous, but a clear warning of his resolve and desperation.

Another trope is the conceit, which endows an insignificant coincidence with meaning. Thus, for example, it is a coincidence that, in his grief for his father's death, Hamlet's eyes are downcast and his father is underground. Gertrude links these two facts in a conceit when she advises him

> *Do not for ever with thy vailèd lids*
> *Seek for thy noble father in the dust.*
> (I.2.70–71)

Conveying as it does the idea that his grief is fruitless, this conceit, though fanciful, requires to be taken seriously. Laertes is also conveying a serious thought when, at the news of his sister's drowning, he exclaims,

> *Too much of water hast thou, poor Ophelia,*
> *And therefore I forbid my tears . . .*
> (IV.7.185–6)

- linking tears with the brook in which she drowned. The fancifulness of this is not proof that he is not serious. What is deplorable about his speech on this occasion is not that he employs rhetoric but that his rhetoric is at fault. Instead of lamenting his dead sister, he parades his grief and makes an exhibition of himself. The first essential of rhetoric is propriety. The speaker must know how to say the right thing at the right time. (Compare with this speech Ophelia's own lament over Hamlet's madness, 'O, what a noble mind is here o'erthrown!' (III.1.152).)

Claudius's very first speech reveals his duplicity. It is a speech full of rhetorical artifice, and it is calculated, but considered in themselves those features are not evidence of bad faith. The aim of the speech is to gain acceptance for his irregular marriage. His duplicity is not revealed by deployment of rhetorical devices, but rather by the employment of devices which sharpen his listeners' awareness of what he is attempting to gloss over. The argument of the first sentence, however gravely phrased, is simply that 'remembrance' of himself is more important to him than remembrance of his brother. (There is a concealed pun upon 'remembrance' here.) He continues:

> *Therefore our sometime sister, now our Queen,*
> *Th'imperial jointress to this warlike state,*
> *Have we, as 'twere with a defeated joy,*
> *With an auspicious and a dropping eye,*
> *With mirth in funeral and with dirge in marriage,*
> *In equal scale weighing delight and dole,*
> *Taken to wife.*
> (I.2.8–14)

This sentence is constructed on the scheme of a 'period'. The reader is kept waiting until the very end for the key word – in this case the verb. Instead of phrasing his sentence: 'Therefore we have taken to wife our sometime sister', he turns the sentence round. The period concentrates attention on the last word, and thus, in this case, on an anomaly. Furthermore he has chosen as a trope 'oxymoron' – a deliberate contradiction in terms. An isolated oxymoron can express a genuine conflict of emotion, as when Juliet, parting from Romeo, exclaims, 'Parting is such sweet sorrow'. But an accumulation of oxymorons, such as Claudius uses here, starting with 'sister . . . Queen', and including the conceit of two eyes, one 'auspicious' and one 'dropping', sounds two-faced.

This is, however, the only time that Claudius commits such an error. His subsequent speeches show him as decisive yet restrained in dealing with the threat of Fortinbras, courteous and friendly with Laertes, and with Hamlet, as he appears in public to the very end, considerate and affectionate. His words are false, but the falsity does not appear in the rhetoric. The general effect of rhetoric is that of a speaker who has made up his mind. In *Henry V* the heroic king shows his courage not in action on the stage but in his rhetoric. Similarly, when Hamlet reappears at the end of the play and drops his antic disposition, his new-found clarity of mind is reflected in his use of rhetoric. The self-possession manifest in 'I prithee take thy fingers from my throat' is no less manifest in his apology to Laertes, even though it contains an elaborate piece of chop-logic which would have delighted Polonius if he could have been there to hear it:

> *Was't Hamlet wronged Laertes? Never Hamlet.*
> *If Hamlet from himself be ta'en away,*
> *And when he's not himself does wrong Laertes,*
> *Then Hamlet does it not. Hamlet denies it.*
> *Who does it then? His madness. If't be so,*
> *Hamlet is of the faction that is wronged.*
> *His madness is poor Hamlet's enemy.*
>
> (V.2.227–33)

This is the speech of the 'scholar, soldier, poet' who has at last recovered himself. His use of rhetoric shows that he is whole. He no longer speaks ambiguously.

His soliloquies, on the other hand, manifest the same excitement that characterizes his exchanges with those whom he despises and distrusts.

Indeed, when he is talking to himself it is just such a character that he is addressing, sometimes at different points in the same speech. Even before he has encountered the Ghost, this dramatic tension is manifest in his first soliloquy.

In this speech, after the court has left the stage, Hamlet gives the audience his own version of the events that Claudius has been referring to, namely old Hamlet's death and his widow's remarriage. The two accounts are very similar in structure. They both involve a long, periodic sentence. Beginning with the words 'within a month', Hamlet's sentence reaches the crucial phrase, 'married with my uncle', only six lines later. Whereas in Claudius's speech the similar interval is occupied by seemly qualifications, in Hamlet's it is occupied by passionate interjections, such as, 'Let me not think on't. Frailty, thy name is woman' (I.2.146). It is as if there were two speakers, not one. Hamlet's passion interrupts him. To add to this drama, before the sentence has quite ended a third speaker appears. An ironical voice is heard, adding a critical afterthought to the denunciation of Claudius: 'no more like my father/Than I to Hercules'.

In his next soliloquy, spoken immediately after the departure of the Ghost, he assumes the role of passionate revenger with an appropriate vow

> *So, uncle, there you are. Now to my word:*
> (I.5.110)

In this speech only one voice is heard. Passion is in sole charge. Afterthoughts are prohibited by Hamlet's vow:

> *And thy commandment all alone shall live*
> *Within the book and volume of my brain.*
> (1.5.102–3)

Before the scene has ended, however, afterthought has begun:

> *The time is out of joint. O, cursèd spite,*
> *That ever I was born to set it right!*
> (I.5.188–9)

All the soliloquies can be analysed as dialogues, involving up to three speakers – a passionate revenger, an ironical malcontent and an actor considering his part. This division matches the different styles of acting required by the stagecraft. Sometimes the actor playing Hamlet presents himself as an actor acting. At other times he represents the

Prince of Denmark, immersed in an intrigue. And there are times when, disassociating himself from the other characters, he joins the audience and criticizes.

In the third soliloquy the separation of these three speakers is startling. Action requires motivation, as Henry V demonstrates in his renowned speech at Harfleur, inciting the English soldiers to

> *Stiffen the sinews, conjure up the blood,*
> *Disguise fair nature with hard-favoured rage.*

In this soliloquy Hamlet addresses a similar battle speech to himself. He has just seen genuine tears in the eyes of the player who recited the Pyrrhus speech. Describing the situation in terms of Hamlet's triple roles, in order to play his appointed role of revenger the actor needs the same facility of feeling, and goads himself accordingly with the player's example. The passion he requires, however, is not pity but rather the wrath exemplified in the portrait of Pyrrhus avenging his father's death. (Interestingly, there is a similar ambiguity in the play-within-the-play, because although the poisoner repeats the crime of Claudius in pouring infection into his victim's ear, he also sets Hamlet an example in choosing his uncle as his victim.)

The actor whips himself into a fit of wrath, in a process lucidly formulated as it is being executed. The player, says Hamlet, had achieved tears by 'forcing his soul to his own conceit' – 'conceit' here signifying 'conception'. The actor similarly wishes to 'force his soul', and uses rhetoric on himself to do so. The opening thirty-three lines are not excited, but calculated. He even taunts himself. In due course the revenger is duly conjured up, replacing the actor with the outburst, 'Bloody, bawdy villain!' The ironist, however, quickly finds this preposterous, stepping in to put a stop to it with cool contempt: 'Why, what an ass am I!'

The revenger remains silent in the fourth soliloquy, 'To be, or not to be', while the actor explores the role of the malcontent. No emotion is expressed. Although the fear of death is referred to, it is not shown. No mention is made of Hamlet's situation, although in the previous scene he has just devised his plot to catch the conscience of the King, and in the next scene he is to spring his trap. The thought is not even directed to sustained consideration of any one problem. Different lines of thought intersect and disappear, with puns serving as points to switch the train of thought from one line to another. For this reason, any attempt to treat this passage as the exposition of a consistent argument involves the listener in ignoring the most obvious meaning of some part of it.

The basic problem is the connection between the opening question – 'To be, or not to be' – with the fear of death. What does the question mean? It may, of course, mean no more than 'To live, or not to live'. There is, however, a different meaning that is no less valid. 'To be' can be taken to mean much more than merely being alive. To really 'be' you must be *somebody*, an active rational being – in short, a man, as Hamlet proudly reminded Horatio his father was a man: 'I shall not look upon his like again' (I.2.188). This meaning of 'to be' was common intellectual currency at the time the play was written. The being of a thing was its essence – which, in its derivation from the Latin word *esse*, 'to be', literally does mean 'being'. To *be* therefore involved realizing one's essence, which called for moral effort. 'Being' involved being true to oneself, as Polonius enjoins Laertes:

> *This above all: to thine own self be true,*
> *And it must follow, as the night the day,*
> *Thou canst not then be false to any man.*
> (I.3.78–80)

This notion has an obvious relevance, which the fate of Laertes himself makes clear. In surrendering to his passion for revenge, and sacrificing his honour to it, Laertes fails to be true to himself, and – as he confesses before he dies – plays Hamlet false.

The foregoing is clearly an acceptable reading. Nevertheless, the other reading is equally acceptable. The words can also be taken to mean 'to live, or not to live'. The application of this reading is, however, itself ambiguous. It is clear that the main reason offered for continuing to live is the fear of death, rather than life's attractions. If life is only a field of 'heartache', and 'natural shocks', the only rational act is suicide, the deed with a bare bodkin that only fear of death prevents.

By the time the soliloquy has reached its conclusion it is clear that more than one kind of action is prevented by the fear of death, and description of these abortive projects as 'enterprises of great pitch and moment' might even seem to exclude suicide altogether from being one of them. What is more important is that the world must be more than a field of 'heartache' and 'natural shocks' if it offers scope for 'enterprises of great pitch and moment'. It must also be a field for heroism.

The deed with a bare bodkin that the fear of death prevents cannot therefore be singled out. It can be either of two quite incompatible deeds – one of self-destruction, one of self-assertion. This incompatibility is encapsulated in the ambiguity of the word denoting the aim of the deed

– 'quietus'. 'Quietus' can be pacification, or it can be the discharge of an obligation. Dispassionately exploring the maze of these implications, the ironist is not looking for the right direction. Instead he questions the very value of any sort of movement, while accepting that immobility too is painful.

In the next soliloquy the Ghost's commandment appears to have been vindicated by the proof of Claudius's guilt, and, consciously linking himself with the powers of evil, the actor uncritically assumes the revenger's role:

> *'Tis now the very witching time of night,*
> *When churchyards yawn, and hell itself breathes out*
> *Contagion to this world. Now could I drink hot blood,*
> *And do such bitter business as the day*
> *Would quake to look on.*

> (III.2.395–400)

The ironist who mocked the cry of 'Bloody, bawdy villain!' is conspicuously absent. The language is borrowed from the melodrama where he has found his 'cue'. This is no less evident in the next soliloquy, where he postpones the killing of Claudius for a more sinister occasion – 'Up, sword, and know thou a more horrid hent' (III.3.88).

In Act IV, however, when Hamlet speaks his final soliloquy, the ironist has returned. In many ways, the occasion is a repetition of that at the end of Act II, when Hamlet was envious of the player's tears. In this case he is envious of the fortitude of Fortinbras and his soldiers, who can 'go to their graves like beds'. The object of the actor is not, however, to whip up his own wrath, but rather to protect himself against second thoughts, by the reflection that reflection is 'one part wisdom/And ever three parts coward' (IV.4.42–3). Thoughts ought to be 'bloody'.

There is ample scope here for irony, and it is exploited to such effect that the speech is often quoted as if its intention were the opposite of its declaration that true greatness consists in finding 'quarrel in a straw/When honour's at the stake'. The expression of the thought undermines it with consistent irony. The example set by the marching men is described as being 'gross as earth'. The spirit of Fortinbras is said to have been 'puffed' with 'divine ambition'. The heroes are deceived: they are risking their lives for 'a fantasy and trick of fame'.

There are no more soliloquies. When Hamlet returns from his journey, the dialogue of actor, revenger and malcontent is over. The actor has found his role. His new certainty is reflected in his unequivocal speech

which, until he is on the point of death, is no longer directed straight at
the audience. Nevertheless its integrity marks a striking change because,
throughout the first four acts, Hamlet has used three voices not only in
his soliloquies but also in his dialogue with other characters upon the
stage, engaged in the action. One of these voices belongs to the actor
himself. Let us call him 'the prince'. The other two voices belong to two
conventional roles that he is tempted to play.

Parts

The absence of any illusion of reality on the stage does not deprive the characters who are being played on it of credibility. To be credible on the stage a character has only to be a recognizable stage presence. Thus the Gravedigger in *Hamlet* is immediately recognizable as one of the stock characters, each with his or her allotted role, who Hamlet declares will be welcome when Rosencrantz and Guildenstern tell him that they passed the players on their way to Elsinore:

> *The clown shall make those laugh whose lungs are tickle o'th'sere.*
> (II.2.323)

Although Claudius may be more than a stage hypocrite, and Gertrude more than a strumpet, like all the other characters in the play – apart from Hamlet himself – they are elaborations of stock models.

All that is required for a character of this kind to remain credible is adherence to an established pattern. From the opening scene, when he comments on Marcellus's story about the behaviour of cocks at Christmas time –

> *So have I heard and do in part believe it*
> (I.1.166)

– to the final scene, when he advises Hamlet, before the fencing match –

> *If your mind dislike anything, obey it*
> (V.2.211)

– Horatio plays the role of the sage counsellor. This makes him so credible a presence on the stage that background inconsistencies which would have reduced him to the level of a spurious concoction in a novel go unregarded in the theatre. When the performance is over, and the text is available to be pondered, a host of questions can be asked about him. For example, in the same scene (I.2) where, reporting the sighting of the Ghost to Hamlet, he states that he saw the dead king once, he also claims:

> *. . . I knew your father.*
> *These hands are not more like.*
> (I.2.211–12)

What holds the audience's attention, however, is not the question of how he can claim to have known the dead king so well if he only saw him once. What concerns them is his continuing attempt to convince Hamlet of what he has seen. During a performance, the other kind of inconsistency is only noticeable when attention is drawn to it in the course of the action – as in the scene when Hamlet inquires how his informants could recognize the Ghost if it was armed from top to toe.

Even variations in Horatio's apparent status do not affect his credibility. In the opening scene, he is treated with some deference by the soldiers (whose own rank, as between that of officer or sentry is similarly questionable from scene to scene) – because the action hinges on the display of the Ghost to a figure of some authority. In his eulogy of Horatio before the performance of *The Mousetrap*, however, Hamlet describes him as a humble person, without revenue. In Act IV, on the other hand, Horatio appears as the adviser of the King and Queen because the only other candidate for the role is Osrick, who could not play it without destroying the credibility of his role as fop. In the final scene, despite the suggestion earlier in the play that he is only a visitor to Denmark, Horatio becomes the spokesman for the whole court when Fortinbras arrives – because he is the only person on the stage who can speak for the dead Hamlet. None of these variations in his status affects his credibility, however, because he is still playing the same role. Something very different happens at the end of the play, however, when the action involves him in an attempt at suicide. The gesture is necessary, but it is also incredible, because it involves abandoning the role to which he has hitherto been narrowly confined.

Hamlet, on the other hand, can switch roles without losing credibility even in the middle of a scene. By the time he has reached his third soliloquy, at the end of Act II, he is stepping in and out of three distinct stock roles – the noble prince, the malcontent and the revenger. (Because of the depth to which he carries it, in Hamlet's case the role of malcontent is incompatible with that of the revenger.) Whether the audience is disappointed or dismayed to see him do so depends upon which role he adopts. But they never cease to believe in him – the actor behind the roles – because his stage presence is different from that of the other characters. He enjoys a special relationship with the audience which releases him from constraints that confine other characters.

Special relationships are typical of the theatre. The villain in a melodrama, for example, is the only character on the stage to whom, by hissing at him, the audience directly express their feelings. If he also takes them into his confidence in soliloquies and asides, so that they know his schemes in advance, he turns them into his accomplices. No matter how fiendish his plot may be, they cannot disclaim their knowledge. They share a secret with him which the rest of the characters do not know, and so have a special link with him, although they may not sympathize with his villainy.

Hamlet's special relationship with the audience is partly of this kind. He does not take even Horatio into his full confidence, but he hides nothing from them. This does not mean that they see all the other characters – Ophelia for instance – from his point of view, but it does involve a special sympathy. This effect is intensified when Hamlet plays the fool. There is a pact between the fool and the audience, that he will mock the other characters for their entertainment if they will laugh in return. When the audience laugh at a laughing-stock – Polonius, for example, detaining Laertes as he bids farewell to him (if the actor plays the scene for laughs) – their laughter is not a tribute to Polonius. When Hamlet makes a laughing-stock of Polonius, however, every laugh is a reward to Hamlet personally:

POLONIUS ... *Will you walk out of the air, my lord?*
HAMLET *Into my grave.*
POLONIUS *Indeed, that's out of the air.* (Aside) *How pregnant sometimes his replies are!*

(II.2.206–9)

This exchange is reinforced because, by means of an aside, Polonius himself attempts to establish a confidential relationship with the audience, thus making an even bigger fool of himself.

But Hamlet's peculiar link with the audience goes even further. Some roles disassociate an actor from the other players and place him on an equal footing with the audience. For example, although the opinions about the other artists which he expresses are all part of the show, the compère stands apart from the other artists in a variety show, and addresses the audience one-to-one. Even closer to a one-to-one exchange is the case of the stand-up comic, confiding fictitious personal opinions and family secrets. In his soliloquies Hamlet discusses topics which concern the audience no less than they concern him, in a manner suggesting that the action of the play itself has been temporarily suspended. The opening words of his third soliloquy – 'Now I am alone' – also mean 'Now *we* are alone'. They are a signal that he has temporarily abandoned the play in order to commune with the audience. The relationship thus established is so immediate that when he observes:

> *I have heard*
> *That guilty creatures sitting at a play*
> *Have by the very cunning of the scene*
> *Been struck so to the soul that presently*
> *They have proclaimed their malefactions*
> (II.2.586–90)

– it seems as if he has designs not on Claudius's conscience but on that of someone sitting at that moment in the stalls.

This effect is not only the result of his soliloquies. It is also the result of the incidental comments to which the action prompts him. Owing to its length the text is usually cut. It can even be cut to the extent that – with the exception of the famous soliloquies – practically nothing remains that is not directly germane to the development of the plot. For example, in Act I, after he has spoken with the Ghost, before he has finished making his companions swear not to reveal what has happened, he incongruously indulges in satirical mimicry of the behaviour of people who contrive to keep a secret while at the same time giving others to understand that one exists:

> *That you, at such times seeing me, never shall,*
> *With arms encumbered thus, or this head-shake,*
> *Or by pronouncing of some doubtful phrase,*
> *As 'Well, well, we know', or 'We could, an if we would'*
> (I.5.173–6)

This passage is often cut. Its satirical stance is hard to reconcile with the rest of Hamlet's behaviour in the scene. But this is true of many other stances he adopts at different moments throughout the play. He shifts from one stance to another in the same scene. If the text is cut so extensively that he is immersed in the immediate action, the audience is offered *Hamlet* without the prince. The prince is an actor.

When the play ends, Horatio is to tell Hamlet's story from a 'stage', to which his body will be borne by four captains:

> *For he was likely, had he been put on,*
> *To have proved most royal.*
>
> (V.2.391–2)

The assimilation of the roles of king and actor is appropriate because, whatever their private feelings may be, both are called upon to play a predetermined role in public, regardless of the circumstances. So it is that Marvell represents Charles I on the scaffold as an actor:

> *That thence the Royal actor borne*
> *The tragic scaffold might adorn:*
>   *While round the armed bands*
>   *Did clap their bloody hands.*
>
> *He nothing common did or mean*
> *Upon that memorable scene:*
>   *But with his keener eye*
>   *The axe's edge did try.*

The king proved his nobility on this occasion by his public performance. The claim is not that he felt no fear, but that he did not betray any. He acted like a king.

Moving as he does in a different theatrical space from that of the other characters, Hamlet can take on a role and put it off, without losing credibility. His role is that of an actor who does not settle into any consistent part until the end. His shifts became mercurial as the crisis develops, but they are essential to the play – and not least when they are most incongruous.

Each time the Ghost appears Hamlet invokes heavenly protection. Nevertheless, the role of noble prince is not a specifically Christian one. This does not mean that his exclamation is worth no more than an atheist's damn. His incidental remarks provide ample evidence of orthodox beliefs about the mechanism of the universe, including the operation of Providence. Salvation, however, is not his aim. His belief in the efficacy of Christian rites and practices only intensifies his hatred of Claudius, because his murdered father died without the benefit of them. It inflames him to damn his uncle as well as kill him. Seeing Ophelia with a devotional text in her hand he confesses:

> *I am very proud, revengeful, ambitious, with more offences at my beck*
> *than I have thoughts to put them in, imagination to give them shape, or*
> *time to act them in.*

> (III.1.124–7)

But this is not humility. His consciousness that such fellows as he have
no business crawling between heaven and earth is desperate. It is
unaccompanied by any hope of forgiveness. The thought that the
Everlasting has set his canon 'gainst self-slaughter deters him from
committing suicide, but only for prudential reasons. The knowledge that
the Everlasting has also forbidden revenge suffices only to make him
hesitate. A nobleman might well owe it to his ancestors to damn himself.

Even at the end, when he acknowledges that Providence had a hand in
his escape from the trap that Claudius had placed him in, his values are
still not Christian. The role of 'Hamlet the Dane' which he has returned
to Elsinore to play is that of a noble prince who pays no heed to the
admonition, 'Blessed are ye, when men shall revile you, and persecute
you, and shall say all manner of evil against you, falsely, for my sake'. If
with his dying breath he stops Horatio from committing suicide it is not
because the Everlasting has fixed his canon 'gainst it, but to ensure that
somebody will survive to vindicate his name.

It is what is 'nobler in the mind' that concerns him in his fourth
soliloquy, just as it is 'a noble mind o'erthrown' that Ophelia laments at
the end of the ensuing scene:

> *The courtier's, soldier's, scholar's, eye, tongue, sword,*
> *Th'expectancy and rose of the fair state,*
> *The glass of fashion and the mould of form,*
> *Th'observed of all observers*

> (III.1.152–5)

Nobility is more than a display of superiority over other people –
although according to Elizabethan belief it partly comes by birth, and in
his third soliloquy Hamlet upbraids himself as 'a rogue and peasant
slave' for his dishonourable inaction. Nobility is a question of knowing
no master – in other words, of independence.

In the first place, this entails a superiority over passion such as
Charles I displayed in his deportment on the scaffold, as Marvell
describes it. He laid his head on the block as easily as if it was a pillow,
thus demonstrating the quality of *sprezzatura* extolled by Castiglione in
his *Book of the Courtier*: 'a certain nonchalance, which conceals all

artistry and makes whatever one says or does seem uncontrived and effortless'. Nor is this merely a question of style. Passion cannot be relied upon, either as a guide or as a motive. In the words of the Player King:

> *What to ourselves in passion we propose*
> *The passion ending, doth the purpose lose.*
> (III.2.204–5)

Control of emotion, however, does not in itself establish nobility. Cunning schemers may possess it, but the schemer is no less a slave than the passionate man. He is dependent upon circumstances. When he seems dexterously to manipulate them, he is in fact subservient to them. The truly noble man is not calculating but careless, as Hamlet is nobly careless before the final fencing match when he does not stoop to check the foils. Claudius had been counting on this:

> *... He, being remiss,*
> *Most generous, and free from all contriving,*
> *Will not peruse the foils, so that with ease,*
> *Or with a little shuffling, you may choose*
> *A sword unbated ...*
> (IV.7.133–7)

As the words 'ease' and 'shuffling' indicate – not to mention Claudius's readiness to exploit a nobility he himself acknowledges – nothing is lower than cunning and deception, however well they may succeed.

As Cleopatra says of the all-conquering Octavius:

> *'Tis paltry to be Caesar:*
> *Not being Fortune he's but Fortune's knave*
> *A minister of her will.*

Such is the ignominious role of Claudius. In his desperate attempts to master events he dances to their tune. Indeed, he lowers himself to the level of Rosencrantz and Guildenstern, who jokingly but truthfully declare their allegiance to the strumpet goddess Fortune – 'her privates we'. The futility of this service is pictured diagrammatically in the traditional image of Fortune's wheel twice referred to in the text. Those who tie themselves to it may rise at the start but are inevitably brought low in the end. In the words of the Player King:

> *Our will and fates do so contrary run*
> *That our devices still are overthrown.*
>
> (III.2.221–2)

When his last device has failed, we have the ignominious spectacle of Claudius desperately scrambling for his life.

> *Take thy fortune.*
> *Thou findest to be busy is some danger.*
>
> (III.4.33–4)

– Hamlet admonishes the corpse of Polonius, the man who sought 'by indirections to find directions out'.

Fortune enslaves men. When Hamlet praises Horatio for his equanimity (in Act III, Scene 2) he does so because he is not

> *. . . a pipe for Fortune's finger*
> *To sound what stop she pleases.*
>
> (III.2.80–81)

It is as ignoble to yield to the despondency or elation resulting from a mischance or a stroke of luck as it is to yield to lust or rage, which reduce a human being to the ignoble level of a beast.

There is thus a surprising but intrinsic similarity between a noble prince and an actor: they both have set parts to play, regardless of internal or external pressures.

One test of nobility is fidelity – remaining faithful to a person, or the memory of a person, when there is no advantage and even a disadvantage in doing so. The courtiers in Act I, Scene 2, fail to pass this test. The late king has been forgotten. Although as yet there is no suggestion of her adultery, Gertrude's infidelity to her late husband's memory, if not to his person, is already flagrant. As his mourning signifies, the only character on the stage who remains faithful to his father's memory is Hamlet. For this he still deserves to be deemed 'the mould of form' even if he is no longer 'the glass of fashion'. Nobody may be following his example, but if he appears eccentric that is because the general behaviour of the court is abnormal. His continued mourning is not an outrage but a valid reproof.

The exemplary propriety of his deportment in the opening scene needs emphasizing. He is not some sort of rebel, flouting convention on a state occasion by appearing improperly dressed. It is the rest of the Danish Court whose behaviour is a breach of convention. The death of the late king occurred less than two months ago, and despite Claudius's adroit attempt to gloss over the situation, his marriage to his brother's widow so soon afterwards is both incestuous and precipitate. Hamlet's role in this opening scene is what it will be in the final scene – the noble prince, 'Hamlet the Dane', the heir apparent. If his dress causes offence, the offence lies in the attention which it draws to royal impropriety.

It draws this attention mutely, however, without itself breaching propriety. Hamlet's deportment may imply a condemnation, but it does not speak it. Claudius can overlook the studied contempt which his nephew shows him, because it never oversteps the limits of decorum. He manifests his disapproval by speaking only when he is spoken to. Then he answers as briefly as possible, but not with open rudeness, employing instead an irony that allows Claudius to save the situation by treating the snub Hamlet administers (by pointedly emphasizing that it is his mother's request that he obeys) as unforced compliance with his own wishes. In public Hamlet is still playing the role of the model prince. It is not until he is alone that he reveals to the audience that he has another role – the malcontent.

The gist of his public performance as a noble prince was to show disdain for his uncle. He has not yet learnt, however, that his uncle is a murderer, and now he is alone it is his mother upon whom his hostility is concentrated. Claudius is only mentioned incidentally, for his inferiority to his predecessor. Hamlet's grievance is against his mother's scandalous remarriage. His description of her response to his father's attentions to her suggests that she fed upon him gluttonously, like a parasite. 'Frailty, thy name is woman.' This misogyny is characteristic of the malcontent.

Although as yet Hamlet has received no cue to play that role, it is also characteristic of the revenger. There is no intrinsic incompatibility between the roles of revenger and malcontent. As a bawd or strumpet is usually involved in the wrong that has to be avenged, most revengers have occasion to echo the Ghost's later observation (so similar to Hamlet's at this point) that:

> . . . *lust, though to a radiant angel linked,*
> *Will sate itself in a celestial bed*
> *And prey on garbage.*
>
> (I.5.55–7)

The revenger may therefore devote as much of his energy to denunciation of women as to murder.

In Hamlet's case, however, after the Ghost's disclosure, there will be an incompatibility between the roles of revenger and malcontent because the latter's disillusionment goes so deep that it makes action of any kind seem futile. The strumpet is the malcontent's own mother, and his reaction to her shameful behaviour is disgust for the very life he owes to her. In Tourneur's *The Revenger's Tragedy*, the bastard Spurio reflects:

> *Adultery is my nature.*
> *Faith, if truth were known I was begot*
> *After some gluttonous dinner – some stirring dish*
> *Was my first father . . .*

In Hamlet's first soliloquy a similar response extends to the wish that his 'sullied flesh' might melt. (His flesh is sullied because, according to the belief then current, he had received it all from his mother while his father supplied the spirit.)

Nevertheless, as appears from Laertes' warning to Ophelia in the next scene, whatever may be the case with the malcontent the noble prince is still a wooer. His letter to her, which belongs to this period, although Polonius produces it in the second act, is a frank declaration: 'I love thee best, most best'. To read the rest of the letter in which these words occur as mockery is to misconstrue it. Some of the beliefs Hamlet cites in the letter as being less certain than his love may already have been dubious in select intellectual circles when *Hamlet* was first staged, but even forty years later, Sir Thomas Browne could still cite disbelief in the motion of the sun as evidence that some people would disbelieve anything. As for the word 'beautified', when the letter was written this carried no pejorative implications.

Nor is the bald style a parody. The letter is written with the plainness which, at the time the play was written, was a fashionable reaction against elaborate locutions, such as those employed by Polonius. The remark that the dead king 'was a man', with which he responds to Horatio's praise of his father, shows that Hamlet can be laconic when expressing his deepest feelings. As for referring to his body as 'this machine' – a commonplace comparison at the time – if this also implies a certain world-weariness, world-weariness is not incompatible with a desire for sexual partnership.

Therefore, although he declares 'the uses of this world' to be 'weary, stale, flat and unprofitable', when we first see him Hamlet's discontent is not disabling. He is not yet aware that, even before his father's death, his mother had already committed adultery with Claudius. His keeps his discontent to himself, as it is unbecoming to a noble prince:

> *But break, my heart, for I must hold my tongue.*
> (I.2.158)

Castiglione claimed to have discovered 'a universal rule which seems to apply more than any other in all human actions and worlds, to steer away from affectation at all costs'. Just as they both have the same brisk style of wooing, Hamlet has Henry V's gift of retaining his authority without losing the common touch. This he proceeds to demonstrate in his frank and easy welcome of Horatio and Marcellus when at the conclusion of his first soliloquy they present themselves to him.

Comparison of Hamlet with the warrior king can be carried even farther. Before his coronation, Henry too did not behave with invariable propriety.

PRINCE *Before God, I am exceeding weary.*

POINS *Is't come to that? I had thought weariness durst not have attached one of so high blood.*

PRINCE *Faith it does me, though it discolours the complexion of my greatness to acknowledge it.*

Even after his coronation, his soliloquy before the battle of Agincourt reveals him still to be, like Hamlet, an actor playing a role, and finding it a heavy burden. And, like Henry V, Hamlet does his duty: 'Go, bid the soldiers shoot.' The last tribute he receives in the play is a salute of guns. The role of noble prince includes that of soldier.

The play opens on a military note with the sentries. These are the men the Ghost has chosen to reveal itself to. They perform their duties without ceremony, straightforwardly and punctually –

> *You come most carefully upon your hour.*
> (I.1.6)

– although the appearances of the Ghost have made them jumpy, and Francisco admits to being sick at heart. When the Ghost does appear, Marcellus courageously volunteers to strike at it, but waits for the order from Horatio before doing so. The note sounded is one of straightforward loyalty. At the end of the scene, the sentries readily fall in with Horatio's suggestion that the matter should be reported to Prince Hamlet – not to the King. They are the prince's friends, not the new king's.

Nothing could be less military than the court in the second scene. Claudius is not a soldier. The only discussion of the threatened invasion is in terms of diplomacy, and later in the play, when Laertes and his followers break into the palace, Claudius relies on a bodyguard of foreign mercenaries ('my Switzers'), not Danish soldiers. This conveys a sense of the existence of two parties at Elsinore, one – the military – incorruptible and dutifully remembering the old king, the other corrupt and subservient to his successor. On the Ghost's summoning Hamlet to accompany it, Marcellus immediately springs to the conclusion that something is rotten in the state of Denmark and proceeds to keep the incident a secret, as he has vowed to do as a soldier and Hamlet's friend.

Hamlet understands soldiers, is at ease in their company, and respects them. The warmth of his greeting to Marcellus, in the second scene, contrasts with the coldness of his treatment of the court in the immediately preceding action, and when he appears on the platform he is obviously at home and knows how to behave – not least when he scorns death and cries:

> . . . *Unhand me, gentlemen.*
> *By heaven, I'll make a ghost of him that lets me!*
> (I.4.84–5)

Fortinbras is not the only warlike prince in the play.

It is therefore evident that plotting revenge in secret is not the only course open to Hamlet when he learns of his father's murder. Long before they have heard that he is much loved of the people and seen from the example of Laertes how a revolt could be started in Denmark, it is clear to the audience that he has no need to act alone. When his friends ask him what has passed between him and the Ghost, a straightforward course lies open for him to take, and when he refuses to tell them he is turning his back on them – a point made theatrically clear by his collaboration with the Ghost *against* them, when he makes them swear secrecy. The physical action implies a connivance which shuts them out, leaving an impression of a man deliberately – even ungratefully – isolating himself from his well-wishers.

After this, until he sees the army of Fortinbras on the march, Hamlet is neither seen in the company of soldiers nor does he give them a thought. This negative fact, however, has its positive significance. Soldiers have been excluded from the general condemnation which, in his discontent, he has passed on the rest of the world during the interval. He never reviles them.

With the word 'murder' the Ghost gives Hamlet his cue to play the revenger:

> *Haste me to know't, that I, with wings as swift*
> *As meditation or the thoughts of love,*
> *May sweep to my revenge.*
>
> (I.5.29–31)

These words echo the boasts of Ariel and Puck, proclaiming their efficiency to their masters. As a revenger he ceases to be a noble prince and becomes a slave. It is a role in which he cannot take even his trusty friends into his confidence. Even later in the play, in Act III when he at least confides in Horatio, the only assistance he seeks from him is in verifying the Ghost's disclosure. The role of revenger is an evil one, as Hamlet has already made plain by invoking hell as well as heaven and earth in his second soliloquy. It is also ignoble. Hamlet has to keep his project secret not only to protect himself against his enemies but also because his designs cannot withstand the scrutiny of a friend.

There is a noble way of righting a wrong without judicial assistance. The scene where the Ghost enjoins Hamlet to avenge his murder with the injunction:

> *If thou did'st ever thy dear father love . . .*
> (I.5.24)

can be compared with the scene in *Much Ado About Nothing* where Beatrice enjoins Benedick to prove his love for her. In both cases the proof demanded is the killing of a wrongdoer. Benedick's honourable reaction is to challenge the offender to a duel. Hamlet's vow of revenge binds him to something dishonourable. It requires the offender to be paid back in his own coin. The aim of revenge is not to cure an evil but to requite one atrocity with another.

Before Hamlet himself commits an atrocity, two theatrical performances have demonstrated the ambiguous nature of his undertaking. The gruesome figure of Pyrrhus, in the player's recitation, is that of a son doing what Hamlet has sworn to do – revenging the death of his father. Lucianus, in *The Murder of Gonzago*, the play within the play, is admittedly not an avenger, but like Hamlet he is bent on murdering his uncle, and his invocation of the powers of darkness will be echoed by Hamlet in due course.

This is because the death of the offender does not in itself satisfy the thirst for revenge. A 'murder most foul' has to be revenged by one as foul. Thus the only consideration that prevents Hamlet from murdering Claudius when he is defenceless, on his knees at prayer, is that it would be too good an end for him. The Ghost's detailed account of the horrors of King Hamlet's death, which Hamlet recalls at that moment, amounts to a demand that Claudius's death must be no less horrible. The revenger must sink to the same level as his victim.

This is what Hamlet binds himself to, and in doing so he isolates himself from common humanity:

> *Yea, from the table of my memory*
> *I'll wipe away all trivial fond records,*
> *All saws of books, all forms, all pressures past*
> *That use and observation copied there . . .*
>
> (I.5.98–101)

It is not only for that reason, however, that he dismisses his friends.

> *I hold it fit that we shake hands and part:*
> *You, as your business and desire shall point you,*
> *For every man hath business and desire,*
> *Such as it is . . .*
>
> (I.5.128–31)

The note of weariness shows that the role of revenger has already been dropped, a point made clear by his words at the end of the scene, when he is alone again:

> *The time is out of joint. O, cursed spite,*
> *That ever I was born to set it right!*
>
> (I.5.188–9)

This curse of the day when he assumed his 'sullied flesh' echoes not only the curse of Job upon the day when he was born but also his own first soliloquy. It thus marks the return of the malcontent, no longer under control but now liable to break out in public.

The transition from revenger to malcontent takes place in the course of the scene in which Hamlet swears his companions to secrecy about the night's events. No trace remains of the prince, who warned them earlier that night how a single defect could ruin a gentleman's reputation. His excitement is no less 'strange' – to use Horatio's word – than the phenomenon of the ghostly voice beneath the stage. It is not only the business with the Ghost which perplexes his friends. It is his incoherence.

His words are marked by inexplicable shifts of tone and intention. He apologizes when Horatio remarks that his words are 'wild and whirling', only to take up his reassurance that there is no offence with a querulous, quibbling insistence that there is. He picks up Horatio's comment that this is 'wondrous strange' to answer, with the urbanity of an arbiter of manners, 'And therefore as a stranger give it welcome', but there is a hysterical indecorum about his alliance with the 'fellow in the cellarage'.

He also conveys a hint of the 'antic disposition' in which the malcontent is now about to manifest himself when, after teasing procrastination, he reveals the secret which the Ghost has told him:

> There's ne'er a villain dwelling in all Denmark
> But he's an arrant knave.
>
> (I.5.124–5)

He is going to play the fool.

The Ghost is responsible for the release of the malcontent no less than for the awakening of the revenger. Speaking of something very like hell, it warned him:

> I could a tale unfold whose lightest word
> Would harrow up thy soul . . .
>
> (I.5.15–16)

but refrained from doing so. In the event, the tale it had to tell him about his mother sufficed to produce this effect. Describing Hamlet's behaviour when he visited her in her closet, Ophelia tells her father in the opening scene of Act II that he looked 'as if he had been loosed out of hell'. The Ghost revealed more than the fact of the murder. It also revealed Gertrude's adultery.

The 'falling off' on her part which, after stressing his own marital fidelity, the Ghost laments must be adultery. Arguments can be derived from the text to support this – as, for example, the way Hamlet proceeds to accuse Claudius, 'that incestuous, that adulterate beast', of two sexual sins, not one. They can also be derived from the original legend and from Belleforest. A theatre is not a court of law, however, and if the question can be settled by a judgement reached only after the play is over, then to that extent the play is a failure. The audience must know the answer to this question before they witness Hamlet's subsequent treatment of his mother and of Ophelia, and so indeed they do. It is obvious from the behaviour of both Hamlet and the Ghost on their first meeting.

The Ghost's warning to Hamlet not to include Gertrude in his act of vengeance implies that Hamlet has just learnt something about his mother which he did not know before – in other words, something more than her incestuous remarriage. There is no other explanation for it, nor for Hamlet's outburst in his second soliloquy, coupling Gertrude and Claudius on equal terms:

> *O most pernicious woman!*
> *O villain, villain, smiling, damned villain!*
>
> (I.5.105–6)

Later comes his reproach to Gertrude in the Closet Scene, that she had committed an act that

> *... takes off the rose*
> *From the fair forehead of an innocent love*
> *And sets a blister there; makes marriage vows*
> *As false as dicers' oaths; ...*
>
> (III.4.43–6)

His relationship with Ophelia has been transformed. He can no longer act the part of the princely wooer. His next approach to her is in the guise of a complete malcontent:

> *At last a little shaking of my arm*
> *And thrice his head thus waving up and down,*
> *He raised a sigh ...*
>
> (II.1.92–4)

In the original story, Amleth feigns madness so that his uncle will not put him to death as a potential rival. Hamlet's distracted behaviour is of no use to him at all. His eccentricity is compulsive. Both in his guise as malcontent and also as revenger, Hamlet is not himself. His true role, the part which as soldier, courtier and scholar he is well equipped to play, is that of a noble prince who is always master of himself. When he plays the part of a revenger or a malcontent – each of which is gripped by passion – he is truly alienated.

This conclusion does not have to be teased out of the text. Several times before he makes 'a sore distraction' his excuse when begging Laertes' pardon in the final scene, Hamlet has already admitted that he is the victim of a mental affliction. Even when he insists to his mother in the Closet Scene that he is only 'mad in craft', all he claims is 'that I essentially am not in madness'. As he states in his last soliloquy, the injuries inflicted on him by Claudius include:

> *Excitements of my reason and my blood*
> (IV.4.58)

These two forms of excitement run counter to each other. The excitements of his blood stem from the murder of his father, and move him to revenge. Those of his reason are the result of the whoring of his mother and drive his previous disgust to the point of nausea. It is at this point that the role of malcontent becomes incompatible with that of revenger, because it vetoes any form of action. Revenge is a social act. The only possible course for a thoroughgoing malcontent is to become a hermit. Thus, at the end of *As You Like It*, Jaques, the play's malcontent, instead of returning to the Court from exile with the good duke, decides to join the repentant bad duke, in a hermitage. Thus, too, in *Timon of Athens* the disillusioned hero, abandoned by his friends, turns his back on Athens and retires to the woods to live the life of a root-eating beast . His rejection of society is so complete that when an invasion gives him the opportunity to return to the city in triumph he refuses it. Instead he delights to imagine the city ravaged by fire, sword and venereal disease.

In the First Folio, Hamlet's famous fourth soliloquy does not occur in its accepted position, at the beginning of Act III, but as soon as he reappears after the Ghost Scene, in Act II. There is a strong argument in favour of that location. In its accepted place, at the beginning of Act III, just after Hamlet has decided on a course of action, it acts as a diversion. Placed in what is now Act II, Scene 2, after Claudius's consultations about Hamlet, it would presage his ensuing behaviour in that act, and the action of the play does not demand any particular location for this soliloquy. It neither connects with nor refers to any particular incident. Indeed, in describing death as a country from which no traveller returns it notoriously fails to take account of the Ghost's revelations. It is as if the actor had temporarily forgotten about the play, and was meditating on the general issues raised by it. Only when he has finished doing this does he take notice of Ophelia's presence, and join her for the Nunnery Scene (which in the First Quarto as in the other versions of the play immediately follows this soliloquy).

The Nunnery Scene develops the implications of Hamlet's visit to Ophelia in her closet, making it clear that his rejection of her is part of a rejection of all humanity. The malcontent regards the female as an enemy because she ensures the continuation of the species:

> *Why wouldst thou be a breeder of sinners?*
> (III.1.121)

Hamlet demands of Ophelia. Misogyny is discontent's high mead. Thus Timon of Athens instructs the army advancing upon Athens:

> *. . . Let not the virgin's cheek*
> *Make soft thy trenchant sword: for those milk paps,*
> *That through the window-bars bore at men's eyes,*
> *Are not within the leaf of pity writ,*
> *But set them down horrible traitors.*

What Hamlet says to Ophelia rapidly degenerates into accusations which are both commonplace and pathological, but the underlying point remains the same:

> *I say we will have no more marriages.*
> (III.1.148)

In the fourth soliloquy which preceded this scene, alternative, even contradictory, threads of thought and impulse lead into one another and even lie side by side in pregnant ambiguity, but although it is impossible to resolve the soliloquy into a consistent argument, its connection with this scene with Ophelia is clear enough. They both stem from an impulse to put an end to existence. Not that the main issue discussed in the soliloquy is suicide. Suicide is mentioned only as part of a meditation upon death as a form of oblivion. Hamlet does not find death fearsome because it might mean annihilation. He regards oblivion as 'a consummation devoutly to be wished', just as the 'uneasy' Henry IV, burdened with responsibility, envied his poorest subjects their sleep.

Confusion on this point arises when the alternative with which the soliloquy opens – 'To be, or not to be' – is interpreted as meaning 'to live or not to live'. At the time when the play was written *being* meant something more than mere existence. It meant realizing a potential by playing a recognized part in the drama of creation. In the image of the universe which Hamlet sneers at when he describes the firmament to Rosencrantz and Guildenstern as a pestilential congregation of vapours, every creature's being was defined by the part it played in a harmonious whole. Uniquely, human beings were free to reject their roles, but after such an abdication, whether or not they still continued to live, they ceased to be.

This confusion is fostered because in the soliloquy itself the expansion offered in the following lines, 'to suffer ... or to take arms', reverses the order of the two items being compared. 'To be', the *first* of the first two items, is the equivalent of the *second* of the next two:

> ... *to take arms against a sea of troubles*
> *And by opposing end them* ...
> (III.1.59–60)

While 'not to be', by the same token, is the equivalent of

> *to suffer*
> *The slings and arrows of outrageous fortune*
> (III.1.57–8)

instead of opposing them. In short, being means doing, while not to be means a feeble existence as 'a nought without a figure', to quote the Fool's description of King Lear's position after his abdication.

This kind of syntactical displacement is not unusual. At the conclusion of the ensuing Nunnery Scene, Ophelia refers to 'The courtier's, soldier's, scholar's, eye, tongue, sword', which – if the order of mention is insisted upon – makes the tongue the characteristic appurtenance of the soldier. Not to accept that there is a similar displacement here involves accepting that to commit suicide is an 'enterprise of great pith and moment'. On the contrary, enterprises of great pitch and moment are projects such as the one to which Hamlet has committed himself, of avenging his father's murder.

In Hamlet's case, however, the issue is further complicated by the fact that although wreaking revenge on the king, his uncle, is a momentous enterprise, it does not befit him to proceed with it. Revenge, like suicide, is forbidden by the Everlasting. The prospect of an after-life, therefore, undermines more than the project of suicide. It undermines the project of revenge as well. Not that Hamlet shows any sign of fearing torments such as those the Ghost has described to him. What gives him pause is consideration of what dreams may come in the sleep of death. His fear is that instead of being annihilated he will still be haunted by his conscience. As Richard II realized, rehearsing his own past life after his abdication:

> ... *whate'er I be,*
> *Nor I, nor any man that but man is,*
> *With nothing shall be pleased, till he be eased*
> *With being nothing.*

To be eased with being nothing is possible only for a person without a conscience – in other words, one who feels no need to play a role. Hamlet has no wish to play a role but is still conscious of a need to do so. As he confesses to Rosencrantz and Guildenstern, in the first flush of his welcome to them, before he has detected their mission:

> *O God, I could be bounded in a nutshell and count*
> *myself a king of infinite space, were it not that I have bad dreams.*
> (II.2.253–5)

The only vital impulse his nausea for life has left him with, however, is to reject. What role does rejection imply? Hamlet never contemplates becoming a hermit, but he does find an analogous role which enables him to reject the society of Elsinore even while remaining in it – the role of fool. The fool may not be a hermit but he is indisputably an outsider. He is not held responsible for what he says. More than that, as the Duke remarks of Touchstone in *As You Like It*, he can 'use his folly as a stalking horse' to hunt down vice. The tactic is to say or do something foolish in order to provoke a conventional answer or comment, for which one has prepared a rasping retort. It is for the sake of this advantage that Jaques is ambitious for a motley coat. Diogenes himself, the arch-malcontent, sometimes played the fool in the same way, as when he appeared in Athens at midday carrying a lighted lamp, so that when asked what he was doing he could reply that he was looking for an honest man. To be the latter, Hamlet in the course of his fooling observes to Polonius, 'as this world goes, is to be one man picked out of ten thousand'.

The satire which the fool's licence sanctions is not invariably sane. Because of the traditional association of his role with the bawdy it lends itself with facility to the expression of misogyny – witness the performances of Touchstone in *As You Like It* and Lavache in *All's Well That Ends Well*. But Hamlet's warnings to Polonius that Ophelia's virginity is fragile – his description of a dog's carcass as 'good kissing carrion', for example – go beyond Lavache's nastiness, just as his treatment of Ophelia in the Nunnery Scene adds a new dimension to Touchstone's callous treatment of Audrey: 'I press in here, sir, amongst the rest of the country copulatives, to swear and to forswear, according to marriage binds and blood breaks.'

But Hamlet has not entirely abandoned the role of glass of fashion and mould of form:

POLONIUS   *My lord, I will use them according to their desert.*

HAMLET   *God's bodkin, man, much better! Use every man after his desert,*
      and who shall 'scape whipping? Use them after your own honour and
      dignity.

                (II.2.525–9)

This advice on how to treat the players provides a rule of conduct for princes which, when he is playing the fool, Hamlet himself ignores. 'Use every man after your own honour and dignity.' There could be no clearer condemnation of his previous behaviour – unless it is his categorical warning to the players not to mock his own chosen victim, Polonius.

The roles of noble prince and malcontent are incompatible, but he plays both roles in this act. He is not the same man to the denizens of the court of Elsinore that he is to visitors. Until they arouse his suspicion, his treatment of Rosencrantz and Guildenstern displays all the graces of a courtier, and to the players he extends a princely welcome. In neither role does he look like a revenger.

How much time has passed since the end of Act I, when he bound himself to enact revenge, may (or may not) be calculated by comparing periods which are mentioned as having elapsed in Acts I and III, but the use of such internal evidence is notoriously questionable – as, for example, the inference that Hamlet is thirty years old which the Gravedigger's reminiscences in Act V support. The impression that Hamlet has been delaying his revenge does not, however, depend on any such calculation. The audience has formed it before Hamlet draws attention to his own sense of delay at the end of the act. All he has achieved by indulging in strange behaviour is to alert Claudius. His enemy has made all the running so far. Instead of presenting the consequences of his encounter with the Ghost, the scenes which succeed the revelation concentrate on Hamlet's state of mind, and while he saunters first with Polonius and then with Rosencrantz and Guildenstern, the other characters – all conscious or unconscious agents of Claudius – are busy probing him.

The Pyrrhus speech which he commands the player to recite serves as an ambiguous reminder of his commitment. The slaughter of the aged Priam is an act of vengeance. Pyrrhus is avenging the murder of his father, the hero Achilles, just as Hamlet has undertaken to avenge the death of his father, the heroic King Hamlet. The description, however, inclines sympathy to the side of the victim. The sight of the actor's tears of pity, however, affects Hamlet as a comment on his own lack of manifest hate. The initial effect of the arrival of the players is to spur Hamlet the actor to resume the revenger's role.

His third soliloquy, in which he absorbs this impulse, is markedly different from the second, in which he embraced that role, because in it he has one foot out of the play. Despite that fact, it is also unlike the fourth soliloquy already discussed, because he keeps his other foot firmly in it. If he tries roles on only to take them off, he does so to illustrate a discussion with the audience which has been provoked by what they have just witnessed together. The intimacy effected by the opening words – 'Now I am alone' – has already been noted, and it is intensified by the phrase, 'this player here', implying a theatrical experience which they have just shared.

The first part of the soliloquy, indeed, consists of Hamlet putting himself through his paces as an actor in a kind of one-man audition, watching himself in company with the audience in the theatre. First he speaks in his own person, noting how, 'all for nothing', the player had contrived to 'force his soul so to his own conceit'. Then he taunts himself, to provoke a reaction, playing upon himself – to borrow a simile he himself uses twice in Act III – 'like a pipe'. No sooner has he succeeded in rousing himself to a fury, however, than he rounds on himself and mocks himself. At this point, the noble prince takes over, full of disdain for the easy relief of feeling in words, and Hamlet brings himself to heel – 'About, my brains!' – to think practically.

Just as in Act II the noble prince implicitly rebuked himself for playing the fool, when he told Polonius to use every man after his own dignity, so in Act III he implicitly rebukes himself in advance for later taking on the role of the revenger who can

> ... *drink hot blood*
> *And do such bitter business as the day*
> *Would quake to look on.*
>
> (III.2.397–9)

– for the act opens with his advice to the players against exaggerated displays of passion, followed by his eulogy of Horatio for his calmness. It should be noted that Horatio is not lacking in passion but he is not 'passion's slave', and the actor is advised in the midst of his passion to 'beget a temperance that may give it smoothness'. In neither case, therefore, is a lack of passion commended. Passion must, however, stay beneath the rein. The model he proposes at this point, therefore, is totally at variance with his own immediately subsequent behaviour.

His display of passion does not begin immediately with the arrival of the court to watch *The Mousetrap*. For one thing, Horatio is still present. At first Hamlet only indulges in satire at the court's expense. (As is evident in the scene with Osrick in Act V, Horatio shares Hamlet's taste for satire.) Nevertheless, although in his exchange with Claudius when welcoming him, in his comments to his mother, and in his harassment of Ophelia, Hamlet does not exactly play the fool, he still acts the malcontent and his jibes amount to misconduct which can be condoned by the court only because the speaker is no longer held responsible for his own words. His observations – on the emptiness of promises, the brevity of women's love, and so on – are cynical commonplaces, and when the performance has been stopped, it is the satirist who greets Rosencrantz and Guildenstern when they return to tell him his mother has sent for him.

Hamlet then dismisses his true friend Horatio along with his false ones, and, much as Lady Macbeth offered herself as a prey to evil powers, works up a blood thirst. The ensuing soliloquy shows that he has indeed forced his soul to his own conceit. There is an element of self-congratulation in the way he registers his readiness to drink hot blood, although he is assuming a posture which the noble prince would coolly ridicule. The ensuing murder of Polonius, in mistake for Claudius, is the result of abandoning the role he was born to play and plunging into another one.

The promised restraint he exercises over himself in the Closet Scene with his mother, however, results in a reappearance of the noble prince – the actor. Already he has twice compared a human being to a pipe – when he praised Horatio for not being a pipe for Fortune's finger to play on, 'to sound what stop she please', and when he accused Guildenstern of thinking he was easier than a pipe to play on. To explore his own temperament, he has already played on himself like a pipe, in his third soliloquy:

> *Am I a coward?*
> *Who calls me villain? Breaks my pate across?*
> *Plucks off my beard and blows it in my face?*
> (II.2.568–70)

Now he does it to Gertrude, in a series of verbal onslaughts that transform her:

GERTRUDE *O Hamlet, thou hast cleft my heart in twain.*
HAMLET   *O, throw aside the worser part of it,*
    And live the purer with the other half.
    Good night. But go not to my uncle's bed.

To her also his advice is to act a part:

> *Assume a virtue, if you have it not.*

She too is like a pipe, but to be played on by herself:

> *For use can almost change the stamp of nature,*
> *And either master the devil, or throw him out*
> *With wondrous potency.*
>
> (III.4.157–161: 69–71)

The advice is to cast herself in a part and grow into it.

Called to account for the murder of Polonius, Hamlet himself assumes an antic disposition with a vengeance. The antic every king is confronted by, as Richard II insisted, is Death:

> *. . . there the antic sits*
> *Scoffing his state and grinning at his pomp.*

Questioned about his disposal of the corpse, Hamlet's replies from first to last are a series of threatening *mementos mori*.

The actor uses himself like an instrument on which to play a set tune. So does the soldier. To achieve its 'full height' a spirit has to be deliberately 'bent up', as Henry V at Harfleur emphasizes. Doing his duty, the soldier too is an actor playing a part: 'Imitate the action of the tiger . . . Disguise fair nature . . . Lend the eye a terrible aspect . . .' 'We put on a compelled valour,' Hamlet remarks to Horatio, in his letter describing his fight with the pirates (IV.6.17). The laconic style in which the letter is written marks the recovery of the soldier in him, of whose existence Claudius reminds us when he tells Laertes how, hearing the latter's swordsmanship praised by a visiting Frenchman, Hamlet could not wait to cross swords with him.

The significance of this return is explored in his final, sixth soliloquy, on seeing the army of Fortinbras – that exemplary 'delicate and tender prince' – on the march. The conclusion reached is sufficiently obvious, but the argument that leads to the conclusion –

> *My thoughts be bloody, or be nothing worth!*
> (IV.4.66)

– is novel. It completes the process whereby Hamlet comes to see the task of eliminating Claudius as a role to be played, rather than a means of securing personal satisfaction.

It was a Renaissance commonplace that the gifts of 'large discourse' and 'godlike reason' distinguished man from beast. As they were man's defining characteristics they must feature in any truly human behaviour. From this it follows that human behaviour cannot simply be the satisfaction of felt needs:

> *... What is a man,*
> *If his chief good and market of his time*
> *Be but to sleep and feed? A beast, no more.*
>
> (IV.4.33–5)

Thus, in *All's Well That Ends Well*, when – his military pretensions having been exposed – the braggart Parolles resolves:

> *Simply the thing I am*
> *Shall make me live ...*

he reduces himself to the level of a beast.

Not that in order to remain human he should have gone on claiming to be a military hero, which he was never meant to be. He should have reverted to whatever more ignominious role had been originally allotted to him – the role which he should never have vaingloriously discarded in the first place. To return to the role allotted to him is what Hamlet now sees he must do. The oblivion which once tempted him he now perceives to be bestial. The soldiers he is now at last resolved to emulate are not longing to lose consciousness. If they 'go to their graves like beds', it is not in order to make their own quietuses but because dying is included in their parts.

The graveyard scene demonstrates that Hamlet is ready to follow them. In his exchanges with the Gravedigger, whose own view of mortality is so matter-of-fact, he coolly looks death in the eye. The only approach to horror he evinces is a natural distaste at the condition of Yorick's skull:

> *And smelt so? Pah!*
> (V.1.197)

To complete his display of readiness to play his proper part, in his accidental confrontation with Laertes he demonstrates the difference between a soldier and a revenger.

From the moment of his return, Laertes' speeches have been marked by their immoderate hyperbole, which now culminates in his speech in Ophelia's grave, and his action in leaping down into the grave is a foretaste of the unrestrained behaviour which his exaggerated language promises. The sudden appearance of Hamlet brings this process to a head. The contrast between the two in speech could not be starker:

HAMLET   *This is I*
          Hamlet the Dane.
LAERTES   *The devil take thy soul!*
HAMLET   *Thou prayest not well.*

                                         (V.1.253–5)

Neither could the contrast between them in behaviour, as Hamlet's next line –

          I prithee, take thy fingers from my throat.

– makes clear.

This contrast in style rules out any question of Hamlet leaping down into the grave to join Laertes there. The First Quarto, which supplies details of performance missing from the other two versions, provides for him to do so. Nevertheless, that particular stage direction is in blank contradiction to the accompanying text. Hamlet is not competing with Laertes in demonstrativeness.

Later on, when the literal meaning of his words suggests that he is doing so, their irony is unmistakable.

HAMLET   *Dost thou come here to whine?*
          To outface me with leaping in her grave?
          . . . Nay, an thou'lt mouth
          I'll rant as well as thou.
                    (V.1.273–4:278–9)

As he says to Horatio, when he repents this behaviour in the next scene, the 'bravery' of Laertes' grief put him into 'a towering passion'. But, as words like 'whine' and 'rant' make clear, the passion in question was disgust, not grief – disgust at Laertes' exaggeration. The challenge to Laertes to eat a crocodile is obviously spoken in mockery. He feels distaste, but he is not carried away by it.

Nor, in the final scene, is he any longer carried away by his hatred and contempt for Claudius, to whom, for the first time in the play, his behaviour is unreservedly respectful.

KING   *Cousin Hamlet,*
          You know the wager?

HAMLET   *Very well, my lord.*
            Your grace has laid the odds o' th' weaker side.
                                (V.2.252–4)

His apology to Laertes is even more handsome – and sincere. He is only
repeating acknowledgements he has already made in confidence to his
mother and in soliloquy to himself, when he asserts that when he did
Laertes wrong he was not himself.

His stance, in short, is not that of a revenger, but that of a prince who
has returned to Elsinore to perform his allotted task. For the first time he
is seen consulting Horatio without reservation. A question of conscience,
as conceived in this play, is no more a private matter, to be settled by
self-examination, than an actor's role in a play is. 'May I with right and
conscience make this claim?' Henry V inquires of the Archbishop of
Canterbury, and in the same spirit, having acquainted him with the full
extent of Claudius's crimes, Hamlet inquires of Horatio:

            . . . is't not perfect conscience
        To quit him with this arm? And is't not to be damned
        To let this canker of our nature come
        In further evil?

                                (V.2.67–70)

In this connection it is important to examine the effect upon him of
his perception that the hand of Providence has been at work. He does
not rely on Providence for support. What he does is up to him. Indeed,
if he had entered this final test in the belief that Providence would
protect him and reward him with the crown, as the outcome is so
different the play would be a grim comedy, not a tragedy. His trust in
Providence amounts to no more than a conviction that he has been
spared to perform a duty.

What his renewed confidence in Providence betokens is liberation
from the revenger's subservience to Fortune. He no longer feels that he
must somehow manipulate events. All he has to do is watch out for an
opportunity which is sure to present itself. When Horatio reminds him
that news of the executions of Rosencrantz and Guildenstern will soon
arrive from England, he answers calmly, 'the interval is mine'. He is not
stirred to contrive anything. He is ready to act when the time comes, and
that is all that is necessary.

This readiness, of course, is also a soldier's readiness to die. His words
to Horatio on the subject echo those which shame Falstaff and his

ruffians in *Henry IV, Part Two*, when the least imposing of their recruits disdains to buy himself off military service:

FEEBLE   *By my troth, I care not. A man can die but once.*
         We owe God a death. I'll ne'er bear a base mind.
         And't be my destiny, so. And't be not, so. No man's too good to
         serve's prince. And let it go which way it will, he that dies this year is
         quit for the next.

His resolute action, however, involves no retraction of his pessimism. The terms in which he forbids Horatio to commit suicide still imply that death is 'a consummation / devoutly to be wished':

         Absent thee from felicity awhile
         And in this harsh world draw thy breath in pain
         To tell my story.

                                        (V.2.341–3)

In all, six characters die as a result of the suppression or neglect of moral conscience, each in his or her own distinctive way. The case of Hamlet is that of the traditional revenger, prompted, as Hamlet himself says, 'by heaven and hell', but eventually redeemed by the renewal of conscience. Conscience is the distinguishing attribute of his family. His uncle and his mother are plagued by it.

Claudius sacrifices his conscience for the sake of immediate gain, and his awareness that this is so only makes his sin worse:

         O, wretched state! O, bosom black as death
         O limèd soul, that struggling to be free
         Art more engaged!

                                        (III.3.67–9)

The resulting suffering is more apparent to the audience than it is to Hamlet, who sees his opponent's mask drop only once. Even so, the audience's glimpses are kept to a minimum. If Claudius were to engage any more interest, their attention would falter and they would miss the point. As it is, his hypocrisy is at times almost admirable, as towards the very end, when his plan has begun to go wrong, he still has the coolness to observe to Gertrude, with apparent pride, 'Our son shall win.' For this reason he has to be deprived of the advantage of soliloquy. The first signal of his guilt is given, very oddly, in an aside. The aside is odd because, unlike most asides, it is not called for to enhance or inform the audience's appreciation of the dialogue it accompanies. When the stage of the Nunnery Scene has been reached, it is time the audience knew that, although he performs so smoothly as a king, Claudius has a bad conscience. As his guilt is a secret, there is no character in whom he can confide. If, in a soliloquy, he confided in the audience, he would be invading Hamlet's territory. An aside is the only solution:

> *How smart a lash that speech doth give my conscience!*
> *The harlot's cheek, beautied with plastering art,*
> *Is not more ugly to the thing that helps it*
> *Than is my deed to my most painted word.*
> *O heavy burden!*

> (III.1.50–54)

The next similar revelation is more impressive, but still not delivered to the audience, being a preliminary to attempted prayer. The only kind of soliloquy Claudius is permitted is that of the traditional villain, revealing his secret plans for the audience's benefit. This occurs at the end of Act IV, Scene 2, when, left alone upon the stage, he reveals the fate that awaits Hamlet in England.

His role is thus deprived of sympathetic interest, for the benefit of the play as a whole. Apart from the reminder contained in his warning to Laertes about the pains resulting from an unfulfilled intention, we have to remember his internal suffering without further help. The only expression of suffering he is allowed is distress when things go wrong. 'When sorrows come, they come not single spies,/But in battalions' (IV.5.79–80).

Being a politician, he does not recognize the hand of Providence. It is only in the next world that he expects punishment. In this world he retains some hope until his very last gasp. 'O, yet defend me, friends. I am but hurt' (V.2.318).

The case of Gertrude is different. At first her poise if anything exceeds that of Claudius. She can talk apologetically about her 'o'erhasty' marriage, and appeal to her son to be more sociable. The play-within-the-play leaves her conscience unscathed – 'The lady doth protest too much, methinks' (III.2.240). Once her conscience has been roused, however, it not only remains active but also causes her a continuous uneasiness, guilt manifesting itself in anxiety, particularly at Ophelia's death. Unlike Claudius, she does expect to be punished in this world:

> *To my sick soul, as sin's true nature is,*
> *Each toy seems prologue to some great amiss.*

> (IV.5.17–18)

The family of Polonius is not much troubled by conscience. Instead each in a different way is governed by a sense of propriety. Polonius himself is a hardened cynic, but because he acts foolish wise man to Hamlet's wise fool we tend to overlook this, and regard him as an entertainer who somehow gets out of his depth. In addition to the stock comic role of a sententious busybody, however, he has the other stock role of the villain's menial. He is proud to be a trusty tool.

The wisdom upon which he prides himself is a hotch-potch of the pious and the prudent. The warning against borrowing and lending, in his homily to Laertes, is contained in the same sentence that tells him how one may not be false to any man. Whereupon, next time we see him, he is instructing his agent to lay 'slight sullies' upon Laertes in Paris. The observation that pricks Claudius's conscience –

> *'Tis too much proved, that with devotion's visage*
> *And pious action we do sugar o'er*
> *The devil himself*

(III.1.47–9)

– is his own gloss upon his own practice. He is interested only in devices.

Conscience does enter the moral life of Laertes, but only at the very end. Unlike Hamlet, who investigates the veracity of the Ghost, he accepts Claudius's account of his father's death without question. He does not think about what to do, but does the done thing. Thus, whereas the cynical Polonius warns Ophelia against Hamlet because he thinks that all young men are unscrupulous lechers, Laertes warns her because he believes that, whatever his inclinations, a prince does not marry beneath him.

In the same way, when news of his father's death reaches him he knows exactly what a man in his position is supposed to do, and procures a poison to 'anoint' his sword. Honour demands satisfaction, and nothing else matters:

> *To hell allegiance! Vows to the blackest devil!*
> *Conscience and grace to the profoundest pit!*
> (IV.5.133–4)

Claudius, who knows his man, chooses just the right terms with which to commend his folly, telling him he speaks 'like a good child and a true gentleman' (IV.5.150). When called upon to wreak vengeance, a gentleman is required to act in a manner which would normally be unbecoming.

Foul play, however, does not come easily to Laertes. Claudius has to take his hand and place it in that of Hamlet, as a lying token of reconciliation before the treacherous fencing match. Even before he receives his fatal wound he has already begun to repent, and declares his action to be 'almost against my conscience'.

In the case of Ophelia, conscience is replaced by filial obedience. Unlike Juliet or Desdemona, she cannot encourage a suit of which her father disapproves. She also appears to be of less independent mind than her counterpart in the original story of Amleth: the woman who, in Belleforest's version, had once loved Hamlet agrees to act as a decoy to discover his secret, but does not give him away. Ophelia shows no compunction about being used as a decoy, so that her father and Claudius can spy on Hamlet. The business may be disguised with professions of concern for the victim's welfare, but the effect of treachery remains. Her obedience makes her passive, not virtuous.

The death toll includes Rosencrantz and Guildenstern. The principle that governs their behaviour is sanctimoniously propounded by the former to Claudius:

> *The single and peculiar life is bound*
> *With all the strength and armour of the mind*
> *To keep itself from noyance . . .*
>
> (III.3.11–13)

They are parasites, a fact guilelessly acknowledged by Guildenstern when he claims to speak to Claudius on behalf of those 'that live and feed upon your majesty'. They are, as Hamlet tells them, sponges, and so it is not surprising that they should be indistinguishable. They play indispensable parts in the pattern of moral obligation displayed by the dramatis personae. Shakespeare introduces them at an early point in its development for that reason. In the original legend they do not appear on the scene until Amleth's uncle appoints two attendants to accompany him on his voyage to England.

The revenge plot metes out justice to all the characters. Those who survive, however, also contribute to the moral pattern, if only by the negative achievement of not having failed in their obligations. The most exemplary character is Horatio. He is Hamlet's friend, not his tutor. One of his functions is simply to endorse the audience's sympathy with Hamlet. When we see him separated from Hamlet's company – with the soldiers on the platform in the first scene, and in attendance on the king and queen in the first of Ophelia's mad scenes – it is clear that he is generally regarded as a man of admirable sagacity. His unswerving friendship for Hamlet is therefore reassuring, and prevents all but the most ingenious of critics from regarding the prince as a centre of infection in an otherwise sane society.

As a friend, he never passes a moral judgement upon Hamlet's behaviour, and indeed he has little occasion to do so. Hamlet's errors are made in Horatio's absence. Until the final scene, the only role in which Horatio ever sees Hamlet is that of the actor, pondering his part. Before transforming himself into a revenger and declaring his readiness to drink blood, Hamlet sends 'good Horatio' out of the chamber. His stance, and the philosophic calm which Hamlet praises in him, make a dramatic comment on the ethic of revenge which does not need to be made explicit.

Another implicit comment is offered by the triumph of Fortinbras. Fortinbras has never acted against his conscience, but his father's defeat and death have been avenged, the losses suffered by Norway have been more than compensated, and the entire family of the killer has been exterminated. Moreover, Fortinbras has been obedient to duty without forfeiting his honour. His voice, at the end, combines the notes of courage, competence and generosity.

The most striking of the unspoken but convincing condemnations of revenge is conveyed by the disappearance of the Ghost that gave it shape. It does not reappear, as its counterparts do in other instances, to gloat over its enemy's punishment. Old Hamlet's death is never even mentioned in connection with the death of Claudius, which appears as retribution for his attempt to murder young Hamlet, and it is on the latter attempt that theatrical interest is focused in the final scene.

Most striking of all, the dying Hamlet makes no reference whatsoever to his father's death. Twice, it is true, his words echo earlier declarations of the Ghost's, but in both cases they only serve to show how far he has gone beyond those declarations. When he adjures Horatio, 'If thou didst ever hold me in thy heart', he recalls the Ghost's adjuration to him at their first encounter: 'If thou didst ever thy dear father love . . .' The service called for, however, is survival. Other words contain an even more significant echo. The stern, elementary horror of the world of revenge is embodied in the Ghost's account of the after-life:

> *But that I am forbid*
> *To tell the secrets of my prison house,*

> *I could a tale unfold whose lightest word*
> *Would harrow up thy soul . . .*

> (I.5.13–16)

The form used by Hamlet in the following passage is very similar, but
the unspoken message is clearly the opposite of harrowing:

> *Had I but time – as this fell sergeant, Death,*
> *Is strict in his arrest – O, I could tell you –*
> *But let it be.*

> (V.2.330–32)

Hamlet's indifference to the Ghost at the point of death can be attributed
to the actor, who sees the play with complete clarity now he has
performed his part. Whenever the Ghost appears, however, it is the
revenger who responds to it, and his passions overwhelm him. On the
first occasion he cannot remain standing. On the second occasion, as
Gertrude notes, his hair stands on end. The reaction of the malcontent is
very different. No sooner has the Ghost departed than the malcontent
mocks it as an obviously theatrical device – 'this fellow in the cellarage'.
Subsequently, when the veracity of the Ghost has been established by
the success of *The Mousetrap*, a similar tone is manifest in the words: 'I'll
take the ghost's word for a thousand pound'. It is the tone of a
sophisticated courtier in a comedy, ironically praising an amateur actor's
performance, as Theseus in *A Midsummer Night's Dream* commends the
Lion, as acted by Snug the Joiner: 'A very gentle beast, and of a good
conscience'.

The malcontent's role, however, is no less limited and limiting than
that of the revenger, and this again is a role that Hamlet does not play in
Horatio's presence. His mockery of Osrick is something very different
from his mockery of Polonius or his confrontation with his mother.
Horatio is not present on those occasions when the malcontent expresses
his nausea. The difference between them is well demonstrated in the
scene where Hamlet is beckoned by the Ghost:

HAMLET   *It will not speak. Then I will follow it.*
HORATIO   *Do not, my lord.*
HAMLET   *Why, what should be the fear?*
          I do not set my life at a pin's fee.

> (I.4.63–5)

Horatio may be able to take Fortune's buffets and rewards with
equanimity, but he does not despise the world.

The only exhibition of the malcontent's railing which is witnessed by Horatio occurs at the performance of the play-within-the-play, when Hamlet mocks Ophelia. Hamlet treats Ophelia as a replica of his mother, a mistress of seeming from whom the mask must be ripped. When she inquires whether the Prologue will explain the meaning of the 'show', Hamlet answers with heavy insistence

> *Ay, or any show that you will show him. Be not you ashamed to show, he'll not shame to tell you what it means.*

> (III.2.153–5)

That he identifies himself with this all-knowing interpreter is made clear by his later claim in the same scene:

> *I could interpret between you and your love, if I could see the puppets dallying.*

> (III.2.255–6)

By harassing her with *double-entendres* he succeeds in demonstrating that she understands 'country matters' – a fact later to be made poignantly evident in her mad songs. What he implies in each of their encounters is, however, that she is an adulteress in the making. His declaration of love at Ophelia's burial is a recantation of the role of malcontent.

The role of malcontent is obsessive. So is that of revenger. So is that of the Ghost. But what was old Hamlet like in his lifetime? A model soldier and a model husband, perhaps he was indeed god-like, but what does that imply? A man can emulate Hercules, Hyperion, Jove, Mars and Mercury only if he is a simpleton. The quality we admire in the 'sanguine athletic gods' of antiquity is, according to W. H. Auden, 'the locomotive beauty of choleric beasts of prey'. The pagan deities and heroes are monumentally single-minded. An undertaking to play the revenger's role is also an undertaking to enlist in this company of monomaniacs:

> *Remember thee?*
> *Yea, from the table of my memory*
> *I'll wipe away all trivial fond records,*
> *All saws of books, all forms, all pressures past*
> *That youth and observation copied there,*
> *And thy commandment all alone shall live*

Within the book and volume of my brain,
Unmixed with baser matter.

(I.5.97–104)

Hamlet the actor cannot confine himself to such a role even for the length of the scene in which he takes this vow. What distinguishes him is precisely his range of thought, the freedom of his mind, the absence of any rigid focus. It is this aspect of the part which makes it hard for some critics to acknowledge the full horror of the twin roles of revenger and malcontent also involved in it. The actor, when he steps out of those roles to saunter through the play in his own person, is such a charming and entertaining companion.

When the Ghost appears to him for the second time, Hamlet inquires whether it has come to chide him for his tardiness. We have just watched him stab a form which he took to be Claudius behind the arras. Nevertheless, we know exactly what Hamlet means by tardiness, and why the Ghost finds it necessary to warn him not to forget. Try as he may, the actor cannot play the role of monomaniac for long.

Hamlet's alternation of roles is possible because all the roles involved are conventional. We do not watch Hamlet as we watch a character in Chekhov. Studying him will teach us nothing about how people actually behave, or how their minds work. The play is not exploring psychology, but theatrical conventions. It was not written for a realistic stage, or for naturalistic performance.

This does not, however, mean that it cannot be taken seriously. Theatrical conventions, like other conventions, are worth exploring because they have not been established without cause. Consider, as an example of a conventional character, the knight in shining armour. He figures in a rescue plot. A princess is imprisoned in a dragon's den: the knight kills the dragon, and restores her to her father. This conventional hero and conventional plot may seem to have nothing to teach us. But what if a writer explores these conventions and tells us that, before she became the dragon's prisoner, the princess was bored and lonely in her father's palace, whereas when she became the dragon's prisoner she enjoyed life in the den and became deeply attached to the dragon? The same conventional plot now has a different meaning. The concept of rescue is seen to be more complex than it originally appeared. This perception is not the simple consequence of the new story. It results only when the story is read as a criticism of a conventional plot with conventional characters.

Hamlet, too, plays a trick with a conventional plot, and in so doing questions the ideas which underlie it. The revenge plot is the story of a man who sets out to punish a wrongdoer and, in the process, himself becomes a wrongdoer, so that he has to share in the final punishment. But what if, Shakespeare's version of the plot inquires, before the final punishment is due the revenger has repented?

Tragedy

Immediately before the fatal fencing match, Hamlet has a premonition of disaster, and, very sensibly, Horatio advises him:

> *If your mind dislike anything, obey it. I will forestall their repair hither*
> *and say you are not fit.*
(V.2.211–12)

By this attempt to avoid the inevitable Horatio shows what he has already shown on previous occasions, that although he is the perfect confidant he has not the makings of a tragic hero. He is not noble, he is 'good'. His benevolence and sagacity are never in doubt, but his approach to ultimate confrontations is evasive. ''Twere to consider too curiously to consider so', is his reproving response to Hamlet's speculations in the graveyard. This difference between the two friends is best exemplified in their reactions to the Ghost:

HAMLET   *It will not speak. Then I will follow it.*
HORATIO   *Do not, my lord.*

(I.4.63–4)

But Hamlet is not to be deterred:

HAMLET   *My fate cries out.*
(I.4.81)

It is the hallmark of the tragic hero that he is doomed and he accepts his doom without flinching. Hamlet dismisses Horatio's suggestion that he should avoid the fencing match by pleading unfitness with the words, 'We defy augury'. This does not mean that he does not believe his premonition. It means that he accepts it, and refuses to be intimidated by it. This recognition of necessity is the essence of the tragic experience, which the audience shares with the hero – an experience which Aristotle, in his analysis of tragedy in his *Poetics*, terms 'catharsis'.

Catharsis is a medical term, and means purging. By means of purging, an organism rids itself of noxious substances. According to Aristotle, the presentation of a catastrophe upon the stage evoked the disabling emotions of pity and fear in an audience in such a way that they were purged. His treatment of this process does not explain how it occurs, but the use of the same term in psychoanalysis is illuminating. Catharsis is a healing process. The patient is suffering from a disability caused by a refusal to acknowledge certain emotions which are inherent in his situation. The cure is effected by inducing the patient to become conscious of these disabling emotions and feel them to the full. By openly facing them and undergoing them he is freed from them.

This concept is directly related to the experience of tragedy by I. A. Richards:

> It is essential to recognize that in the full tragic experience there is no suppression. The mind does not shy away from anything, it does not protect itself with any illusion, it stands uncomforted, unintimidated, alone and self-reliant. The test of its success is whether it can face what is before it and respond to it without any of the innumerable subterfuges by which it ordinarily dodges the full development of experience. Suppression and sublimation alike are devices by which we endeavour to avoid issues which might bewilder us.

> (*Principles of Literary Criticism*)

Among the illusions which Richards mentions as obstacles to this bleak, heroic recognition is religious consolation, such as Horatio proffers in his farewell to his dead friend:

> *Good night, sweet Prince,*
> *And flights of angels sing thee to thy rest!*
> (V.2.353–4)

This piety is an expression of affection. It is characteristic of the speaker, but, as far as the audience is concerned, it is beside the point. Throughout the play, death has been presented as a mystery – an 'undiscovered country' – not as a gateway to bliss. Heaven is referred to constantly, but only as the seat of justice – the justice that demands Hamlet's death. Tragedy may have originated in religious rituals, but it developed an independent identity by confronting life in life's own terms, without benefit of an after-life. For purposes of the play, Hamlet's death is final.

It is, of course, true that some people may free themselves from disabling emotions by means of a religious belief or a philosophy, but this is not the tragic way. Tragedy does not free the audience by offering it ideas, but by making it feel to the full, and what is felt to the full is the dreadfulness of the specific situation in which the hero finds himself. The audience's experience is based upon its sympathy with the hero in his catastrophe, their perception that he is doomed. At the final stage of the tragedy, according to Aristotle, this process is clinched when the hero himself comes to see that he is doomed. The plot proceeds to a crisis, at which point 'recognition' occurs. The hero realizes the irreversible truth.

Thus, in the *Oedipus Rex* of Sophocles, the crisis occurs when Oedipus realizes that the man he killed long ago in a brawl was his father, and the woman whom he subsequently married when he became King of Thebes was his own mother. As a tragic hero, to use Richards's words, he 'stands uncomforted, unintimidated, alone and self-reliant', accepts the truth in its enormity, and acts accordingly. The tragic effect is thus entirely the result of the action in which the hero is involved, and the emotions evoked in the audience which are to be purged are pity and fear.

Turning from *Oedipus Rex* to *Hamlet*, two questions arise. Pity and fear were the only two emotions which Aristotle assigned to tragedy, but are they in fact the predominant emotions felt by an audience watching *Hamlet*? And is it indeed the case that the audience responds primarily to the action in which the hero is involved? Notoriously a great deal of Hamlet's attention is devoted not to action but to reflection. Admittedly the play does not offer the audience a philosophy, but it nevertheless contains a wealth of ideas. Aristotle's analysis of tragedy is cogent and must be the starting-point of any consideration of the subject, but it was inevitably limited to the tragedies he knew. *Hamlet* offers an experience similar to that afforded by *Oedipus Rex*, a discharge of disabling emotions, but these emotions are not simply those provoked by his family situation. The negative emotions treated by *Hamlet* are not direct responses to his plight. They are responses to his perception of the implications of his plight – his sense that life is meaningless. The emotion to be purged is neither pity nor fear. It is disgust for life in general.

The peculiar character of *Hamlet* becomes clear as soon as we examine the contribution made by its plot. For Aristotle the plot was central. All other features of a play served only to emphasize the intrinsic interest of the plot. In this respect *Oedipus Rex* is a perfect example of tragedy as he conceived it. At the commencement of the action, the kingdom of Thebes is afflicted by blight and pestilence, and this is taken to be a sign that it contains some polluting presence. Oedipus has been appointed King of Thebes,the previous king having failed to return from a journey; arriving as a stranger, Oedipus had freed it from the persecutions of the Sphinx. It is now his task to free it from the curse under which it is suffering, and he consults an oracle to learn how this can be done. The answer is that the murderer of the previous king is living in Thebes, which will continue to suffer until the murderer is driven out. Oedipus therefore inititates an investigation to identify the murderer, by questioning a series of informants and witnesses. The action leading up to the crisis is a sequence of investigation scenes.

Perturbation begins at the very first stage of the investigation when the sage Tiresias declares, under pressure, that the culprit is none other than Oedipus himself, but this seems unbelievable, and further witnesses are called to prove the accusation is untrue. Each stage of the process seems to allay one suspicion only to give rise to another, until it is finally undeniable not only that Oedipus is indeed the murderer, but also that the murdered king was his own father. When he recognizes the truth, Oedipus, unwilling to look any longer upon the world, puts out his own eyes and leaves Thebes to become a wanderer in exile. The action is therefore composed of a series of interlocked scenes leading up to a final crisis of recognition, at which point the drama is concluded.

Nothing could be more unlike the plot of *Hamlet*. In the first place, in *Hamlet* there is not a single plot but three, so that the organizing centre of the play is not Hamlet's revenge but is something that arises from comparison of three acts of revenge. The audience, therefore, in so far as the action is concerned, is required not simply to respond to what it sees but also to consider its general implications. In the second place the development of Hamlet's revenge is governed not by factors which are already present in the initial situation, as is the case with Oedipus's investigation, but by extraneous circumstances – the arrival of the players, the voyage, the pirates. In the third place, and partly but not entirely as a result of this difference, the scenes in *Hamlet* do not interlock, leading consequentially one into another, as the scenes in *Oedipus Rex* do. Most strikingly of all, whereas the high point of the action of *Oedipus Rex* occurs at the end, the most intense moments of the action of *Hamlet* occur in Act III. Indeed it is impossible to locate a moment in *Hamlet* that corresponds with Oedipus's recognition of his situation. Hamlet learns of his father's murder in the very first act, so that in so far as his situation is that of a man obliged to act in a certain way he recognizes it at the beginning. Further recognitions occur, as when the play-within-the-play confirms Claudius's guilt, or Hamlet comes to realize that there is a providence in the fall of a sparrow. The final recognition is the realization that he has been trapped and poisoned. None, however has the significance of Oedipus's single, catastrophic realization. Moreover, although the situation Hamlet faces is exciting, it is not calculated to inspire fear and pity. If it produces catharsis, the negative emotions which it purges are not those of fear and pity, and it is not attention to the action on the stage that produces it.

Concentration on the action in *Oedipus Rex* does not involve neglect of any aspect of the performance of the central character, but in *Hamlet* it means concentration on a single role – that of Hamlet as revenger. When we consider the full range of the performance of the actor playing

Hamlet, and in particular his peculiar intimacy with the audience, it is immediately apparent that the audience perceives him in a very different light from that which illuminates its perception of Oedipus. There is a total absence of dramatic irony. Dramatic irony results when the audience is aware of crucial aspects of the character's situation of which he himself is ignorant. In *Oedipus Rex*, as the action proceeds it becomes evident to every spectator – not only those in the audience but also those upon the stage – what Oedipus's real situation is, while he remains in ignorance. The chorus becomes uneasy; his informants begin to see the direction in which their evidence is pointing, and beg him to desist in his questioning. His wife, perceiving the truth before he does, leaves the stage to commit suicide. A point is reached where he alone is blind to the truth.

This effect is totally absent in *Hamlet* until the final scene, when the audience knows that Hamlet is trapped, although he himself does not. Up to that point Hamlet knows everything that the audience knows. They know only what he does, and are, indeed, accomplices in his deception of the other characters. They are in a conspiracy together, and Hamlet communes with them directly. The stagecraft made possible by the conventions of the Elizabethan stage gives the play a most unusual dimension, impossible in classical tragedy. It might seem, however, that this dimension is comic. Hamlet operates as a trickster, conniving with the audience in his deception of the other characters, and secretly or openly deriding his enemies in each encounter.

Comic characters are not unknown in Shakespearian tragedy. They contribute to, rather than detract from, the tragic effect. The jokes of the porter in *Macbeth* only enhance the evil atmosphere: he pretends to be the porter who ushers in the damned at the gate of hell. In *Antony and Cleopatra*, when Cleopatra procures an asp in order to commit suicide, it is from a clown whose malapropisms only underline the significance of her action – as when he warns her to be careful of the snake because its bite is 'immortal'. A similar character in *Hamlet* is the Gravedigger or Clown. Like the comic characters in the other tragedies, however, his role is a minor one. What sets *Hamlet* apart from the other tragedies is that there is a strong comic element in the performance of the hero himself.

It is true that the form this takes is in the role of malcontent, but that does not prevent the play from being a comedy. *As You Like It*, which is unquestionably a comedy, features Jaques who is a malcontent; ending as it does in the hero's death, *Hamlet* clearly cannot be compared with *As You Like It*, yet its persistent comic thread, which lasts until the very last scene with the mockery of Osrick, might indicate that to treat the play as a tragedy may be to misconstrue it. If the sequence of scenes does not produce a mounting sense of crisis, is this not because attention is not focused on the plight of Hamlet, called upon to put things to rights in Denmark, but rather to express a vision of Denmark – and thus of the world – as being incorrigibly wrong?

Aristotle maintains that the plot of a play is its life and soul. Other factors of significance – the speeches, for example – are significant only to the extent that they illuminate the significance of the action on the stage. A very different view has sometimes been expressed about the relative significance of speech and action in Shakespearian drama. According to this view, Shakespeare's plays should be regarded not as poetic dramas but as dramatic poems. The poetry is the life and soul of the play. The chief function of the characters is not to act, but to speak, all contributing, in different voices, to a unified poem.

Considered as such a poem, *Hamlet* is an invitation to pessimism. The imagery produces a background of corruption, disease and death. Each character contributes to this pattern, beginning with the sentinel, Francisco, who in the opening passage declares that he is 'sick at heart'. The Ghost adds to this effect by his appearance and, later, by his words – not the information about Claudius, but the general tenor of his grim picture of the hereafter. Horatio's warning of the terror of the Ghost suggests how precarious sanity is. It needs no ghost to fill the mind with deadly thoughts. A precipice suffices:

> *Think of it.*
> *The very place puts toys of desperation,*
> *Without more motive, into every brain.*
> (I.4.74–6)

These 'toys of desperation' are also to be found at court, as the case of Ophelia shows; Gertrude's sadly sinister account of Ophelia's drowning serves to crown this effect. Laertes in his rage speaks of hell, devils and damnation. The players, in the Pyrrhus speech and in the play they perform, intensify the atmosphere. Even Rosencrantz and Guildenstern, when they warn Claudius of the need for self-preservation, present a frightening picture of the wheel of fortune running out of control. Claudius rivals Hamlet in the consistency of his vision of a desperate sickness. Whenever a character lifts his eyes from his immediate circumstances to view the horizon, the vision is black. Only Polonius, who is too busy to see beyond the end of his nose, is immune to the general expression of pessimism.

If this were the sum total of the play, however, it would be nothing but a lamentation, but such a view of it is absurdly incomplete. The characters are not merely members of a chorus. Each has an individual part to play. Moreover, in considering the part of Hamlet, it is ridiculous to consider it only as a speaking part. He is in continuous action. He does not merely soliloquize and nod and wink to the audience. Nor is his suffering merely general. What he generalizes is the anguish of his particular situation.

This tendency to generalize has been held to be the subject of the tragedy which a host of critics have, in different ways, declared to be tragedy of a newer, more modern kind than that of ancient Greece. The element of fate, according to this view, is not an external power but rather something internal – the disposition of the hero, something he cannot help, which operates as a curse in the peculiar situation in which he finds himself. The kind of character presentation which this view entails is not one to which the Elizabethan stage readily lends itself, as we have seen, because it was a stage that did not direct the audience's attention to minute and realistic detail. Nevertheless Shakespeare did contrive to create memorable, rounded characters in whose reality, as creatures with independent life, it is possible to believe. Of these the most famous is Falstaff, but there are tragic characters as well, such as Othello and Coriolanus, of whom it could be said that their tragedy was simply the fate of being themselves. The analysis of the part of Hamlet we have already made precludes any such view of it, but as this psychological view has been taken by a line of interesting commentators, it deserves consideration in order to see where it leads.

The idea, which is tragic in its implications, is that Hamlet's virtues were his undoing in the peculiar situation of being called upon to execute revenge. It was first stated by Goethe.

> A lovely, pure, noble and most moral nature, without the strength of nerve which forms a hero, sinks beneath a burden which it cannot bear and must not cast away. All duties are holy for him: the present is too hard. Impossibilities have been required of him: not in themselves impossibilities, but such for him.
>
> (*William Meister's Apprenticeship*, translated by Thomas Carlyle.)

It is not easy to recognize Hamlet in this picture, but it was brought a little closer to the figure on the stage by Coleridge, who diagnosed 'great, enormous, intellectual activity, and a consequent proportionate aversion to real action, with all its symptoms and accompanying qualities.'

The closest approximation to the figure on the stage was achieved by

A. C. Bradley who, in his diagnosis of the problem in *Shakespearian Tragedy*, links the earlier blow of his father's death and his mother's remarriage to his speculative disposition. Even before the Ghost's revelation, Hamlet has received a 'violent shock to his moral being', which has plunged him into melancholy. Bradley argues that if a sudden demand for violent action were made upon a man already in a state of melancholy,

this state might well have for one of its symptoms an endless and futile mental dissection of the required deed. And, finally, the futility of this process, and the shame of his delay, would further weaken him and enslave him to his melancholy still more. Thus the speculative habit would be *one* indirect cause of the morbid state which hindered action . . .

The distinction of this analysis is that it admits the independence of Hamlet's role as malcontent. Like other kindred explanations, however, it ignores those aspects of Hamlet's part which belong to the soldier Ophelia describes him as being, in addition to the courtier and the scholar.

This objection cannot be raised against the theory of L. B. Campbell (in *Shakespeare's Tragic Heroes: Slaves of Passion*) who is concerned to discover what, in the light of Elizabethan rather than nineteenth-century psychology, is the significance of the tragedy. According to Elizabethan psychology there were four constituents of personality, each conducive to a specific style of behaviour. Ideally these constituents should be evenly balanced, but were usually found in mixtures wherein one 'humour' predominated. Applying Elizabethan description to Hamlet, she finds that he was not melancholic but rather choleric. In support of this finding, she quotes an interesting passage from *The Optick Glasse of Humors* (1607):

They that are of this complection are very affable in speach, and have a gracious faculty in their delivery, much addicted to witty conceits . . . quipping without bitter taunting: hardly taking anything in dogeon, except they be greatly moved . . .

The choleric man is also sociable, and a faithful friend. Such, according to this argument, was the personality of Hamlet, before the noble mind, as Ophelia laments; was 'o'erthrown'.

What overthrew it was the passion of grief. Sir Thomas More divided those who suffer grief into two categories: those willing to accept comfort and those who refuse it. Of the latter there are two kinds, one of which becomes wildly active while the other becomes lethargic. This latter kind is that to which Hamlet belongs:

... so drowned in sorrow that they fall into a carelesse deaddelye dulnesse, regarding nothing, thinking almost of nothing, no more than if they lay in a letarge, with whiche it may so falle, that wit and remembrance will weare awaye, and falle even fayre from them. And this comfortles kind of heavinesse in tribulacion, is the highest kind of the deadly sinne of slouth.

(Sir Thomas More, *Dyalogue of Comforte Agaynst Tribulacyon.*)

These descriptions are interesting not only for the light they throw on psychological thinking at the time when *Hamlet* was written, but even more because they show how imperfectly any description of psychologically consistent behaviour fits the complete part of Hamlet, considered in all its fullness. Just as much of his behaviour cannot be attributed to the speculative sensitive posited by Bradley, so also we cannot recognize the character who mocks Polonius and soliloquizes so brilliantly in the dull, lethargic figure who thinks 'almost of nothing'.

What lies behind these attempts to diminish the multiple and varied performance required of the actor who plays Hamlet? It is the attempt to discover in his character a fatal flaw to which his death can be attributed, instead of attributing it to the requirements of the plot – the need for the revenger to be punished. His death is attributed to a reluctance, or an inability, to kill Claudius. It was this delay which enabled Claudius to plan Hamlet's death, according to the theory, and the delay was Hamlet's own fault.

Hamlet can be said to have delayed throughout the second act, which he spends playing the malcontent instead of the revenger. This delay, however, is not fatal. He has his opportunity to kill Claudius in Act III, when he finds him unguarded and at prayer. It is to this point that any examination must return. It is crucial. It cannot be attributed to any of the characteristics with which these theories endow him; he tells us why he postpones the killing, and the reason he gives does not pertain to a morbid inactivity or sensitivity. He postpones the killing in order to execute a more perfect revenge, in a manner which would be taken for granted at that time. One Elizabethan story, for example, tells how a murderer threatened to kill his enemy unless he uttered terrible blasphemies, and, when the victim had obliged, immediately dispatched him before he had time to repent. It may be legitimate to reinterpret certain features of old plays if they are incomprehensible to a modern audience, but not if such a reinterpretation belies the rest of the play and its procedures. In this case if Hamlet does not mean what he says he is deceiving himself, as he says it only to himself; nowhere else in the play is this his manner in soliloquy. Moreover, in the very next scene he stabs

Polonius behind the arras in mistake for Claudius. There is thus only one instance of fatal delay, and it cannot be blamed on any of the traits that have been designated as Hamlet's fatal weakness.

The question is not why did Hamlet delay, but why did Shakespeare? Why, instead of proceeding directly from the meeting with the Ghost to the play-within-the-play, does he give us an interval (throughout Act II) in which the project of revenge is suspended so that Hamlet can perform as a malcontent? The answer, clearly, is that the role of malcontent, although irrelevant to the revenge plot, is the vehicle of the essential interest of the play. This interest is not Hamlet's reaction to his particular situation. The central interest is Hamlet's pessimism. The focus of interest in the action is not what Hamlet does about his father's murder. It is what Hamlet does with his disgust. The negative emotions which the tragedy produces are not the pity and fear which Aristotle found in Greek tragedy, but contempt and disgust.

It is in this light that Nietzsche sees Hamlet when he allies him with 'the Dionysian man':

... both have once looked truly into the sense of things, they have *gained knowledge*, and nausea inhibits action; for their action could not change anything in the eternal nature of things: they feel it to be ridiculous or humiliating that they should be asked to set right a world that is out of joint. Knowledge kills action; action requires the veils of illusion: that is the doctrine of Hamlet, not that cheap wisdom of Jack the Dreamer who reflects too much ... Not reflection, no – true knowledge, an insight into the horrible truth, outweighs any motive for action, both in Hamlet and in the Dionysian man.

(*The Birth of Tragedy*, translated by Walter Kaufmann)

In other words, Hamlet is a tragedy not of fear and terror, but of disgust. The reason why the act of revenge is delayed is to enable Hamlet to present that disgust so that the audience will share it and experience its purgation in the final scene. It is for this reason that the antics of Act III are interposed between the revelation of the Ghost and the play-within-the-play. It is for this reason that, before the final scene, we are shown Hamlet in the graveyard. And it is also for this reason that, at different points in the action, the other characters express a pessimism matching that of Hamlet, like a chorus of despair.

Knowledge is the term Nietzsche applies to Hamlet's pessimism, his sense of futility, and it is true that if the audience comes to share Hamlet's pessimism – as they must if they are to experience the tragedy – then for a time it must appear to them that his pessimism is justified. They have to feel that his case is not theirs but that they too are involved in it. This effect is essential to tragedy. One of the classical rules of tragedy was that the hero must be a person of high degree, and a reason given for this rule was that the spectacle of a person in an apparently impregnable position subjected to catastrophe inevitably produced the reflection that if even such a personage was not immune to fate, the case of lesser mortals was indeed precarious. In Shakespeare's own day, writing of tragedy in his *An Apologie for Poetry*, Sir Philip Sidney points out that 'with sturring the affects of admiration and commiseration [it] teacheth the uncertainty of this world, and upon how weake foundations guilden roofes are builded'.

In other words, the suffering of the hero was generalized. In *Oedipus Rex*, a chorus representing the common citizens of Thebes generalizes the terror of the hero's fate by expressing its increasing trepidation at witnessing the spectacle of his downfall, and concludes the play with the reflection that no man can be called happy until he has reached the very end of his life without catastrophe.

The negative emotion which is purged in *Hamlet* is not, however, trepidation of this kind, but rather the response that results when – to quote Sir Philip Sidney again – an event 'openeth the greatest wounds, and sheweth forth the Ulcers that are covered with Tissue'. If these ulcers are purely local to Denmark, they will not affect the audience directly. The audience must perceive them as general, and therefore must be presented with a view of life in its entirety that promotes disgust. Hence Hamlet's appalled disgust at the vision of the sun breeding maggots out of a dead dog fails of its purpose if it is regarded as a symptom of mental disease. It must be shared, at the time he expresses it. It will be purged before the audience leaves the theatre.

As this disgust is only temporary, it is in the end replaced by that state which Hamlet calls 'readiness'. If knowledge is the issue, it is not disgust but readiness that expresses it. Even readiness, however, cannot be regarded as knowledge. It is a state of mind in which to meet a desperate situation, not a state in which to live continually. Tragedy does not offer philosophy, but the rectification of specific emotional excesses. Its value is not that it teaches truths, but that it sees us through despondencies to which all men are prone.

If we seek knowledge in *Hamlet* we are bound to misread the play, especially if we believe we know what knowledge is, because in that case we insist that in the end the play must reflect the knowledge we ourselves possess. Either we misread the play by our insistence on discovering in it a confirmation of our own belief, or else we reject it because we are not able to find that confirmation. This difficulty is exemplified in L. C. Knights's treatment of the play in *An Approach to Hamlet*.

'Most certainly,' L. C. Knights concludes, 'Hamlet's way of knowing the world is not Shakespeare's own.' He reaches this conclusion because he regards certain of the tragedies as explorations of ways of knowing, and finds in them the presentation of a process whereby the hero learns to abandon egoism through the development of a free and delicate responsiveness. The brutality of the revenger and the despair of the malcontent alike demonstrate the absence of this sane and sensitive disposition.

The basis of Knights's approach to the play has to be psychological because his concern is with states of mind, and because it is psychological he treats Hamlet's performances, and in particular his performance as revenger, not as explorations of particular conventional roles but as symptomatic of his illness. What is theatrical in these performances, viewed in this light, is evidence of Hamlet's egoism, not exploitation of the conventions of the Elizabethan stage. 'Again and again,' Knights points out, 'intrinsic values, direct relations, are neglected whilst he tries out various roles before a real or imagined audience.' The fact that there is a genuine audience watching in the theatre is thus ignored. Hamlet is acting, in this view, to an imaginary audience. 'His jests and asides imply an approving audience "in the know" and ready to take the point.' But there is indeed such an audience, and it is Shakespeare, not Hamlet, who has them in mind.

When he comes to Act V, Scene 1, Knights registers no change in Hamlet's attitude to death. Instead of noting that resignation to the unalterable fact of mortality has replaced Hamlet's earlier disgust, he finds only a prolongation of a morbid fascination. Hamlet's declaration of his 'readiness' in the next, final scene is therefore regarded as arbitrary and sudden, especially as Knights interprets 'readiness' as being the state of open responsiveness which he believes to be Shakespeare's own way of knowing the world. We have not seen Hamlet achieving this healthy state in the course of the previous action, and cannot therefore feel that he has earned it.

What Hamlet has achieved is not the generally commendable attitude to life that Knights attributes to Shakespeare, but a readiness to act which is a readiness to die, and he earns it in the only acceptable way, by dying. It is for this reason that the catastrophe is inevitable and Hamlet is doomed. The revenger may be doomed by his guilt. The revenger, however, is a subsidiary role. Hamlet's main role is that of malcontent, and this is why he is a universal character. He embodies that sense of futility which dogs human life and is an inescapable part of it, in the same way that Don Quixote embodies the quixotic.

Hamlet does not conform with Aristotle's description of tragedy for two reasons. In the first place, it is designed for a different stage, with a different theatrical tradition. In the second place, the negative emotion which it offers to purge is neither pity nor fear but disgust. The disgust can only be experienced by the audience if it extends beyond the situation in which the hero is placed by the plot, to include the human situation as the audience itself experiences it. This means that the hero has to communicate general disgust, and not confine his attention to the task with which the plot entrusts him. The conventions of the Elizabethan stage enable him to do this by establishing an intimate relationship with the audience, and by the poetic expression of the emotion in the verse spoken not only by the hero but also by the other characters.

The thought that 'all the world's a stage' was an Elizabethan commonplace. The insistent theatricality of the performance does not therefore distract from its seriousness. We may regard it as the tragedy of an actor with a part to play, who starts by trying on two masks, neither of which is appropriate. In the end he finds the mask that fits, but it is too late to avoid disaster. This action is not, however, one that concerns actors alone. We are all called upon to play a part in life, and so we are all actors in our own way. The part is something that has to be carried. 'O, heavy burden!' Claudius groans. 'Who would fardels bear?' Hamlet exclaims a few lines later.

The play affords the purging of this negative emotion, just as pity and fear are purged in *Oedipus Rex*, and we are shown Hamlet's single, final recognition of the plight of humanity in the speech in which he declares himself ready.

Catharsis occurs when the other characters are already dead, and Hamlet is dying, already mourned by those around him. The death is tragic. It meets Aristotle's requirements exactly, in that although it is not entirely undeserved, for Hamlet is guilty, it is unnecessary because the revenger who committed his offence has already vanished. The disappearance of the prince represents nothing but loss:

> For he was likely, had he been put on,
> To have proved most royal.

(V.2.391–2)

(In other words, he would have acted like a prince; let us also note that it is to a 'stage' that his corpse is carried.)

And yet the audience is left with a sense of relief. Not in words, but in the way in which he dies, Hamlet communicates this sense of freedom, a reassurance that might be expressed as a message that the burden can be carried:

> *Had I but time – as this fell sergeant, Death,*
> *Is strict in his arrest – O, I could tell you –*
> *But let it be.*
>
> (V.2.330–32)

Appendix One

Comparison of *Hamlet* with some other Elizabethan Revenge Tragedies*

Thomas Kyd, *The Spanish Tragedy* (*c.*1589)

The revenger in this play is Hieronimo, Marshal of Spain, where he is in attendance at court but not so powerful that he can prevail, by legitimate means, against those who do him wrong. The King of Spain himself is just, but his justice is not available to Hieronimo against his enemies, one of whom is Balthazar, a prince of Portugal (a country with which Spain seeks peace), while the other is Lorenzo, the King's nephew. He thus has to resort to underhand means to make them pay for the murder of his son, which they have committed in secret.

It is not by means of a ghost that the villains' secret comes to light, but nevertheless a ghost does feature in the play – the ghost of Don Andrea, one of Balthazar's previous victims. The performance in fact begins with the appearance of Don Andrea's ghost, recently arrived in the Underworld of Greek legend, who has been brought back to earth by the god or spirit of Revenge himself to see Balthazar receive his deserts. These two characters remain on stage to watch the action of the subsequent tragedy of Hieronimo, occasionally passing comments upon it that serve to emphasize that, however well things may seem to be going for Balthazar at the moment, his doom is certain.

In this way some sense is conveyed of events working themselves out to a predestined conclusion, and reference is even occasionally made, in the course of the action, to Heaven. Nevertheless there is a marked absence of any Christian ethos, such as that which colours, while it may not define, the action of *Hamlet*. Revenge is the theme and it receives little criticism, even at the end, for although the King of Spain is ready to mete out harsh punishment to Hieronimo, who escapes only by committing suicide, the last episode concerns the return of Don Andrea to the Underworld with a promise that he can personally superintend his enemies' torments.

The arrangement for the whole play to be presented as a performance watched within another performance (that of Don Andrea and Revenge), heightens the theatricality of the play, and there is also, as in *Hamlet*, a

*The approximate date of *Hamlet* is 1601.

103

play-within-the-play, devised by Hieronimo, in which his enemies take part in a performance before the court. By this means he devises their deaths, by converting theatrical stabbings into real ones.

Hieronimo's revenge is not immediate, but suffers a delay, like that of Hamlet. The interval is occupied by ingenious malpractice by the villains, and by scenes of injustice, so that the delay might not be noticed were it not for the fact that, like Hamlet, Hieronimo comments on his delay. He justifies it on the grounds that revenge has to ripen.

In a soliloquy which crudely anticipates certain reflections of Hamlet, Hieronimo appears with a book in his hand and comments on certain passages. Such similarity as there is, however, only serves to emphasize the total absence of the intellectual pressure that Shakespeare exercises on the audience through Hamlet's conscience. Moreover, although he occasionally rails against the universe, Hieronimo's sense of injustice is concentrated on his own particular case.

Hieronimo does not feign madness, but he exhibits both forms of genuine madness that feature in *Hamlet*. Crazed by grief for his son's death, he periodically behaves fantastically. Consumed by the rage for revenge, he is prepared to risk damnation to achieve it:

> *Though on this earth justice will not be found,*
> *I'll down to hell . . .*

This is particularly evident in his readiness to make the innocent suffer with the guilty. Although the King and his brother are innocent of his son's death, Hieronimo gloats when, as spectators of the fatal play-within-the-play, they are compelled to witness their own sons' deaths, and thus taste his grief. Before committing suicide, he gratuitously kills the King's brother, dying unrepentant, 'Pleas'd with their deaths, and eas'd with their revenge'.

John Marston, *Antonio's Revenge* (1599)

The hero is Antonio, son of the Duke of Genoa, but the action takes place at the court of Piero, the Duke of Venice. Piero is an arch-villain and the action on the stage is largely occupied by his machinations, which include the frustration of the planned marriage of his daughter with Antonio by a false accusation of unchastity against her. This romantic element in the plot, however, takes second place to a more classic revenge element, although the daughter's death, broken-hearted, in Act IV does give Antonio an additional motive. Indeed his appetite for revenge is sharp enough already, as Piero has murdered his father.

Arriving in the opening scene to serenade his bride-to-be, Antonio learns simultaneously of her alleged infidelity and of his father's death. He is, accordingly, overwhelmed by grief, accompanied by a suspicion of Piero, although he has not yet learnt that the latter is his father's murderer. At this stage his situation is like that of Hamlet before he meets the Ghost. He seeks solitude:

> *I have a thing sits here; it is not grief,*
> *'Tis not despair nor the most plague*
> *That the most wretched are infected with;*
> *But the most grief-full, despairing, wretched,*
> *Accursed, miserable – O, for heaven's sake*
> *Forsake me now; you see how light I am,*
> *And yet you force me to defame my patience.*

His father's ghost informs him of the truth, whereupon this nameless feeling is transformed into a rage for revenge which, like Hamlet, he confirms in a vow to allow no other thought to enter his mind.

Unlike Hamlet, however, he has no difficulty in acting upon this commitment to obsession. There is nothing in his mind – nothing anywhere in the play – to question or counter the primitive ethic of an eye for an eye. Antonio refrains from killing his enemy when he has the chance – in this case, to preserve him for a lingering death – and instead commits a brutal murder. (He kills Piero's innocent and trusting young son.) In Hamlet's case, however, the unnecessary slaying of Polonius was not intentional, although still not innocent. When, again like Hamlet, Antonio visits his mother in her bedchamber, he is prepared to kill her for encouraging the advances of Piero, until his father intervenes. The widow is not credited with a conscience, but on seeing her ex-husband's ghost she is shocked into becoming Antonio's accomplice against Piero.

Indeed the similarities with *Hamlet* serve only to emphasize the extent of Shakespeare's exploration of the implications of the situation. In part this is a function of the hero which Antonio cannot sustain. His feigned madness is a clear instance of this. Hamlet's fooling is an instrument of exposure: he uses it to unmask. Marston, who had a gift for satire, endows Antonio with a general hostility to life, but it remains an abstract hostility, a mere expression of personal misery which ought, he informs his mother, to drive him mad, but does not. In Act IV he disguises himself as an idiot and attends a crucial scene unrecognized. He refuses the role of social critic.

As for the madness of revenge itself, Marston presents it as an uplifting, chastening experience. Before the end of the play, Piero's villainies have turned the senators of Venice against him. After Piero has been cruelly and slowly done to death (in the process of a masque, in which he has been treacherously invited to take part), Antonio and his fellow conspirators are invited to choose what offices of state they will assume. They decline the offer. They would rather commit suicide

> ... *but since constraint*
> *Of holy bands forceth us keep the lodge*
> *Of dirt's corruption till dread power calls*
> *Our soul's appearance, we will live enclos'd*
> *In holy verge of some religious order,*
> *Most constant votaries.*

This trite religiosity illustrates the other reason why this play fails to explore the revenge theme. It has no sense of the Christian values which make human imperfection an ordeal to be accepted and transformed.

As for the comparison of Antonio with Hamlet, it is interesting to note that in the execution of his revenge Antonio is assisted by two other victims of Piero's villainy. One is a courtier, who has acted until this point as a sort of buffoon. The other is a philosophically minded man, who at first attempted to 'suffer' patiently, rather than to 'take arms', but comes to realize that 'Man will break out, despite philosophy'. This team comes near to resembling the part of Hamlet, with its multiplicity of roles.

Cyril Tourneur, *The Revenger's Tragedy* (*c.*1606)

In Tourneur's play the hero, Vindice, has three distinct roles. He is known as himself to his own family, but, as he has been living in retirement from the court, when he appears there he can act like a plain, prose-speaking rustic. In addition, he disguises himself as a pander. Consequently the play bears a resemblance to *Hamlet* in certain elements of comedy and satire which are missing from *The Spanish Tragedy* and *Antonio's Revenge*. Vindice finds the role of revenger so easy that he has ample time to play the malcontent as well.

The play contains no ghost, and, apart from a treacherous masque in the final act, the other usual features of revenge tragedy are missing. Not only is there no feigned madness and no mention of delay, but Vindice is in no danger. Nobody suspects him. There is not even very much he needs to do. In the most literal sense of the phrase, his enemies are their

own worst enemies. They are all members of the family of a wicked
duke, who spend their time planning murders and seductions, both of
one another and of other victims. Vindice simply has to move among
them in disguise, from time to time interposing a fatal masterstroke.

The wrongs to be revenged relate to sexual crimes rather than to
murder. In Act III, the old Duke is trapped and killed because, nine
years previously, he poisoned Vindice's mistress when she rejected his
advances. He is succeeded by his son Lussurioso, who is killed in his
turn in Act V, because he has attempted to seduce Vindice's sister.
Vindice's methods are ingenious and, in their insistence on the
maximum of mental if not physical pain, malicious. This is particularly
so in the case of the old Duke, who is lured to a secret assignation
with what he believes to be a shy new conquest, but is in fact a
dummy rigged up by Vindice. The head is the skull of the dead
mistress, which since her death Vindice has kept as an ornament in
his study but which now serves as a bait. It has been smeared with
poison, which kills the Duke when he attempts a kiss. He dies slowly
enough, however, to be made to witness his wife's adultery with his
bastard son. Vindice also displays a total callousness in his readiness
to see the innocent suffer, when they are wrongly accused of his own
crimes.

Perhaps this last is because they are courtiers and he is essentially a
malcontent. This particular aspect of the revenger's role is fully fledged
in Vindice. The ducal court itself is a sitting target for a satirist. Its
characters are labelled with names that declare their qualities –
Lussurioso is lecherous, Ambitio is ambitious, Supervacuo is inane,
Castiza (Vindice's sister) is chaste. Vindice's own name proclaims him
to be a revenger, which is indeed his part in the plot, but he is more
prominent as a commanding stage presence whom the others obey like
puppets, while he supplies a commentary that is both sinister and comic.
In this he resembles Hamlet, sometimes as fool, sometimes as
malcontent, and the resemblance is most marked when, like Hamlet, he
mocks the theatricality of his situation. At one stage, when Lussurioso
lies outrageously, Vindice asks in an aside, 'Has not heaven an ear? Is
all the lightning wasted?' The question seems melodramatically
rhetorical at this point, but forty lines later, when he is left alone on the
stage and in the course of a soliloquy repeats this inquiry, thunder
obligingly sounds off-stage. This theatrical joke recalls Hamlet's
mockery of the Ghost in the 'cellarage', just as Hamlet's style of fooling
is recalled in passages like this one (in which Vindice is disguised as a
pander):

LUSSURIOSO   *What hast been – of what profession?*
VINDICE   *A bone setter.*
LUSSURIOSO   *A bone setter!*
VINDICE   *A bawd, my lord.*
            One that sets bones together.
LUSSURIOSO   *Notable bluntness!*

When all the wicked characters are dead he announces that he and his brother were responsible, expecting gratitude from the new Duke, but receiving instead the punishment due to a murderer.

As in the case of Hamlet, a madness of disgust that matches the madness of rage is lurking. Rage, it is true, Vindice never exhibits. He is a cool murderer. He does, however, suffer from a preoccupation with lust, death, and the corruption of the spirit by the flesh. Thus, regarding his mistress's skull, he reflects:

> *And now methinks I could e'en chide myself*
> *For doting on her beauty, though her death*
> *Shall be revenged after no common action.*
> *Does the silkworm expend her yellow labours*
> *For thee? For thee does she undo herself?*
> *Are lordships sold to maintain ladyships*
> *For the poor benefit of a bewitching minute?*

As in *Hamlet*, other characters contribute to the prevailing mood. Bent on seducing his father's wife, Spurio, the Duke's bastard son, speculates:

> *Duke, thou didst do me wrong and by thy act*
> *Adultery is my nature;*
> *Faith, if the truth were known I was begot*
> *After some gluttonous dinner; some stirring dish*
> *Was my first father; when deep healths went round*
> *And ladies' cheeks were painted red with wine,*
> *Their tongues as short and nimble as their heels*
> *Uttering words sweet and thick . . .*

In both *Hamlet* and *The Revenger's Tragedy*, there is an accompanying strain of misogyny. Disguised as a pander, Vindice bribes his mother to betray his chaste sister to Lussurioso – to test her. In due course, threatening her with their daggers, he and his brother terrify her into repentance. There is a dash of *Hamlet* in all this, as also in the conclusion; having triumphed over his enemies and boasted of his success, Vindice is sent for instant execution by the new, good, Duke. He reaps as he has sowed, just as Hamlet does.

Unlike Hamlet, however, he is never dissatisfied with himself. He learns nothing. He never changes, and, despite his flippancy and his pessimism, his unchanging face is one of moral superiority and aggression. In its satirical exploitation of the role of malcontent, Tourneur's play comes nearer than other revenge tragedies to *Hamlet*, but it does not begin to explore that role in depth.

George Chapman, *The Revenge of Bussy D'Ambois* (c.1610)

The roles of revenger and malcontent alike are warped by passion. Hamlet earns his tragic status by undergoing that process of distortion and then emerging, tempered by the ordeal, as a prince. He passes through a period of ignobility in order to become noble. His victory is rewarded by detachment, but it comes only at the end, when he has learnt the truth about the roles of malcontent and revenger by playing them and meditating upon them. In *The Revenge of Bussy D'Ambois*, on the other hand, the hero, Clermont, is noble from the start, and detached as well. The roles of malcontent and revenger do not tempt him, and he has no need to meditate because he has thought everything out already, before the action starts.

Quite simply, he is not a dramatic character because he is above the level of any tense or problematic relationship. This even applies to his relationship with himself. He does not have to choose among roles. He is not pulled in different directions. It is obvious that a considerable intellect has been brought to bear in the writing of his speeches, but their interest is negligible when compared with those of Hamlet. However general it may be, Hamlet's thought gains an extra dimension from its context in the play. Clermont merely utters general truths, which appear, in his case, to be of such power that he is incapable of suffering. He is, in fact, a Stoic.

His philosophy makes it impossible for him to make a malcontent's mistakes because he believes that any perception of imperfection must be partial, and therefore erroneous. Viewed from the point of view of the whole, everything is in its proper place, and therefore as it should be. We know that this is what he believes, not because he has at any point to remind himself, but because he is always willing to give good advice, and the other characters delight to listen to him.

Disgust is therefore out of the question. It is interesting to compare his impassive pronouncements on the subject of sex with Hamlet's revulsion at 'incestuous sheets':

> *. . . what excites the bed's desire in blood*
> *By no means justly can be construed love,*
> *For when love kindles any knowing spirit,*
> *It ends in virtues and effects divine,*
> *And is in friendship chaste and masculine.*

In the same way, he is not subject to the passions that transport revengers. Nevertheless, he recognizes an obligation to avenge the death of his brother, Bussy D'Ambois (the hero of a previous tragedy by Chapman), because the culprit is beyond the reach of justice in terms of the law. In this view, revenge is a moral duty.

As a moral duty cannot involve the infringement of moral law, and this means that the law of the land must not be broken, revenge is difficult to achieve, even though Clermont regards duels as legal between noblemen. His brother's murderer declines the challenge. His sister grows impatient, and so does his brother's ghost, who chides him for delay. In the end Clermont does stoop so far as to gain surreptitious entry to his enemy's home, and the duel takes place. It is fought strictly according to the rules and ends with his enemy's death, whereupon Bussy and other ghosts enter and dance about the victim's corpse.

Clermont commits suicide. Much of the action has not been occupied by the revenge plot but by court intrigue, and no sooner has Clermont avenged his brother's death than he learns that his great friend, the Duke of Guise, has been murdered at the instigation of the King. There is no course left to him but death:

> *There's no disputing with the acts of kings:*
> *Revenge is impious on their sacred persons.*

Appendix Two: Texts

Before it appeared in the First Folio of 1623 ('F', the first collected edition of Shakespeare's plays), *Hamlet* had already appeared in two earlier Quarto versions, the First Quarto ('Q1') in 1603, and the Second Quarto ('Q2') a year later.

Q1 is markedly different from the other two versions. In the first place, it is much shorter: 2,154 lines, as against the Q2's 3,723. More significantly, where lines from Q2 and 'F' correspond they are in the main identical and where they differ they still match each other closely, whereas in Q1 the similarity of corresponding lines is often only approximate. Moreover, any resulting difference in quality is almost invariably in favour of the later versions.

This difference was once accounted for by the theory that what was printed in Q1 was an earlier text – not the *Ur-Hamlet* but an earlier version by Shakespeare of the text later printed (with only comparatively minor variations between them) in Q2 and F. Detailed examination of the omissions and differences does not support this hypothesis, however. In the first place, sections of the later versions which are missing from Q1 are often discursive passages such as would be cut in order to produce an abbreviated acting version of the very long complete text. Some of these missing sections are also absent from F, presumably for the same reason. The additional omissions in Q1 might be explicable as further cuts, perhaps aimed at producing an even shorter version of the play for a provincial tour.

Some of Q1's omissions, however, do not merely abridge the Q2 text: they mutilate it. Nor do Q1's mutilations stop short at omission. Many passages are rewritten in a rough-and-ready approximation to blank verse that cannot be compared with the relevant passages in Q2 and F. To take the opening lines of Hamlet's fourth soliloquy as an example:

> *To be, or not to be – that is the question;*
> Whether 'tis nobler in the mind to suffer
> The slings and arrows of outrageous fortune
> Or to take arms against a sea of troubles
> And by opposing end them. *To die, to sleep –*
> *No more –* and by a sleep to say we end
> The heartache and the thousand natural shocks

111

> That flesh is heir to. 'Tis a consummation
> Devoutly to be wished. To die, to sleep –
> *To sleep – perchance to dream. Ay there's the rub.*

Cutting the non-italic passages to shorten the play would produce –

> *To be, or not to be – that is the question.*
> *To die, to sleep. No more.*
> *To sleep – perchance to dream. Ay there's the rub.*

What Q1 offers, however, is the following –

> *To be, or not to be, I there's the point.*
> *To Die, to sleepe, is that all? I all:*
> *No, to sleepe, to dreame, I mary there it goes . . .*

This is clearly not Shakespeare's earlier version of the Q2 text but a defective memory of the Q2 text, patched out with rough-and-ready substitutions. A faulty memory is also the simplest explanation of other features of Q1, such as passages which differ from corresponding passages in Q2 only in that although employing the same words, they jumble the order.

Add to such considerations the fact that Q1 also contains phrases from other plays, and it becomes clear that Q1 is not based on a text but on an actor's memory. Those scenes in which he played a part are those which are reproduced most accurately. When it came to scenes in which he did not appear, he had to use his own invention to versify the précis which was all his memory supplied.

This explanation of the vagaries of Q1 has gained general acceptance as a result of the analysis made by G. I. Duthie in *The 'Bad' Quarto of Hamlet* (Cambridge, 1941). It does not, however, rule out the possibility that the reporter's memory may have been of a slightly different and earlier version of the play. For example, in Q1 the fourth soliloquy and the Nunnery Scene occur in the second act, not in the third. Polonius and Reynaldo have different names – Corambis and Montano. After the Closet Scene the Queen becomes Hamlet's active ally, in league with Horatio against Claudius. The idea of poisoning the unbated foil in the plot against Hamlet originates with Claudius, not with Laertes. As the reporter's treatment of the text demonstrates that where he could not remember he had no scruple in fabricating, these minor differences could, however, equally plausibly be attributed to a faulty memory combined with a readiness to improvise. Unless further textual evidence of its existence is discovered, the hypothesis of an earlier Shakespearian version is unprovable and, by the same token, has no practical consequences.

J. Dover Wilson's argument that the 'good' Quarto (Q2) was printed from Shakespeare's own manuscript, or 'foul papers', *The Manuscript of Shakespeare's 'Hamlet' and the Problem of Transmission* (2 vols., Cambridge, 1934) is generally accepted. Unfortunately, however, this manuscript was evidently not perfectly legible, so that Q2 contains an unusually high proportion of misreadings and guesses on the part of the compositors. These sometimes can only be remedied by editorial conjecture, but in the first instance they call for checking against the other two texts – not only F but also, despite its manifest defects, Q1. Indeed, in their difficulties, the compositors of Q2 themselves evidently consulted Q1, as can be ascertained by comparison of Q2 with the later F text, for the latter sometimes supplies the correct word which a compositor of Q2 demonstrably replaced with an incorrect word from Q1 because he could not read it in the manuscript.

Not that F is always preferable in Q1 in such cases. Take, for example, the passage where Hamlet warns Rosencrantz of the ultimate fate of Claudius's agents:

> *He keeps them like an ape an apple, in the corner of his jaw, first mouthed to be last swallowed.*

> (IV.2.17–19, Penguin edition)

In the opening clause, Q2 omits the ape and F omits the apple, whereas 'He keeps them as an Ape doth nuttes', is Q1's version.

Moreover Shakespeare's foul papers clearly did not give complete stage directions. F, which is believed to have been based on a prompt-copy of the play, makes more adequate provision in this respect, but the actor-reporter who provided the material for Q1 from his recollection of performances is sometimes even more generous. In the final scene, for example, the stage directions in Q1 are the only ones which include the essential detail that Laertes wounds Hamlet. (Q2 does not even mention the exchange of rapiers.) Sometimes, too, Q1 offers a stage direction with its own peculiar value. When the mad Ophelia enters, Q2 merely offers, 'Enter Ophelia'. F has 'Enter Ophelia distracted'. Q1, however, recalls 'Enter Ophelia playing on a Lute, and her hair downe singing'.

In view of its provenance, however, Q2 is the text on which a modern editor bases his edition, correcting it where necessary by reference in the first place to F. Q2 is the fuller version. F, being a text for performance, features cuts, although not to the same extent as Q1. There are 230 lines included in Q2 that are missing from F, most notably Hamlet's final soliloquy on seeing Fortinbras's army on the march, but also several other passages which, although contributing nothing to the plot, heighten the significance of the action – starting in the first scene with the long speeches leading up to the appearance of the Ghost, and ending with the bulk of the scene between Hamlet, Horatio and Osrick in the last.

On the other hand, F also includes material which is not to be found in Q2, to the extent of some seventy lines in all. Some of these omissions in Q2 are manifestly the result of careless printing. Thus, in the graveyard scene, the compositor's eye demonstrably skipped from one occurrence of the word 'arms' to another lower down, with the result that the intervening words were omitted. (V.1.33–7) Other omissions are harder to explain. Abridgement to reduce performance time is not a likely explanation, as the passages in question were retained in F, which has clearly been abridged for that very purpose. There may have been particular reasons for censoring Hamlet's observations on Denmark and imprisonment (II.2.239–69) or Rosencrantz's report of the success of the boy players (II.2.336–61), but they can only be conjectured. What is certain is that the existence of such discrepancies means that none of the three contemporary published versions can be ignored in the task of assembling an authentic text.

The editor is posed a particularly interesting problem by material presumed not to have originated with Shakespeare but developed by the actors in performance. Q1 contains such embellishments, in particular a passage censuring clowns in Hamlet's advice to the actors, excluded by most editors, but included by Anne Barton in the Penguin edition (III.2.43–55). In F they abound. Such interpolations present an interesting question. It is a common theatrical experience that a play grows in rehearsal, and even in performance, with the consent of the dramatist. Any such additions to Shakespeare's foul papers would not appear in Q2. Thus, in F, and to a lesser extent in Q1, Hamlet has a characteristic trick of repeating a word or phrase:

HORATIO.   *It would have much amazed you.*
HAMLET.   *Very like, very like.*

(I.2.235–6)

If it was not Shakespeare but Burbage who attached this mannerism to him, did Shakespeare endorse it? The Penguin edition allows it to remain. The Arden editor removes it. Similar treatment is accorded to the cry 'O vengeance!' which occurs half-way through Hamlet's third soliloquy in F but not in Q2, and to Hamlet's playful cry of 'Hide fox, and all after', at the end of the scene where Rosencrantz and Guildenstern demand to know what Hamlet has done with Polonius's corpse.

Every scene in *Hamlet* is the product of a series of editorial decisions. Two major ones have already been discussed (pp. 69 and 78) – the location of the fourth soliloquy together with the ensuing Nunnery Scene, and the question whether Hamlet leaps down into the grave to grapple with Laertes or Laertes leaps out of it to grapple with him.

Throughout the text, however, there are significant questions calling for answers, witness the discrepancies between the three texts in the opening passage of the Closet Scene (III.4) up to the entry of the Ghost. For a start, F cuts six lines of expostulation from Hamlet's part as given in Q2 (lines 72–7; 79–82.) But the questions posed by omissions are easily answered, if the intention is to regain Shakespeare's text. Different criteria must be invoked to settle discrepancies such as the following.

In Q2, lines 49–52 read:

> . . . *Heaven's face does glow*
> *Ore this solidity and compound mass*
> *With heated visage, as against the doom,*
> *Is thought-sick at the act*

whereas in F they read:

> *Yea this solidity and compound mass*
> *With tristful visage* . . .

Here a choice has to be made between heavenly and earthly thought-sickness, and between heat and sadness. A similar choice has to be made between two versions of lines 91–2. F's version is:

> *And there I see such black and grained spots*
> *As will not leave their tinct.*

Q2's version is:

> *As will leave there their tinct.*

In the first case *leave* means 'lose', and in the second 'deposit'.

Then there are stage directions. The sound of Hamlet's voice, within, calling out to his mother when the scene opens (line 6 in the Penguin edition), features only in Q1 and F. Is it to be omitted, as an actor's addition? And should a stage direction then be inserted to indicate that Polonius hides behind the arras, when all the texts leave this to be inferred?

Q1 comes into its own in the stage direction for the entry of the Ghost, by adding the striking detail, missing from Q2 and F, that the Ghost is 'in his night gowne'. The contrast with the apparition's previous appearance that this domestic touch supplies is significant and moving, preparing the audience for the concern for his distraught wife which the apparition is soon to show – matching her own concern for her apparently unhinged son.

These are only the chief discrepancies of over forty which occur in this brief passage.

Suggestions for Further Reading

Landmarks

Bradley, A. C., *Shakespearian Tragedy* (London, 1904)

Bullough, Geoffrey, *Narrative and Dramatic Sources of Shakespeare* (Vol. 7) (London, 1968)

Campbell, Lily B., *Shakespearian Tragic Heroes: Slaves of Passion* (Cambridge, Mass., 1930)

Coleridge, S. T., *Coleridge on Shakespeare*, ed. T. Hawkes (Harmondsworth, 1969)

Eliot, T. S., *Selected Essays, 1917–32* (London, 1932)

Granville-Barker, Harley, *Prefaces to Shakespeare: Third Series, Hamlet* (London, 1937)

Jones, Ernest, *Hamlet and Oedipus* (London, 1949)

Knight, G. Wilson, *The Wheel of Fire* (London, 1930)
    The Imperial Theme (London, 1931)

Schucking, L. L., *Character Problems in Shakespeare's Plays* (London, 1922)

Spurgeon, Caroline F. E., *Shakespeare's Imagery and What It Tells Us* (Cambridge, 1935)

Williamson, C. C., *Readings on the Character of Hamlet 1661–1947* (London, 1950)

Wilson, J. Dover, *What Happens in 'Hamlet'* (Cambridge, 1935)

General criticism, which includes a study of Hamlet

Battenhouse, R. W., *Shakespearian Tragedy: Its Art and Its Christian Premises* (Indiana U.P., 1969)

Bayley, John, *Shakespeare and Tragedy* (London, 1981)

Clemen, W. H., *The Development of Shakespeare's Imagery* (London, 1951)

Collick, John, *Shakespeare, Cinema and Society* (Manchester, 1989)

Edwards, Phillip E., *Shakespeare and the Confines of Art* (London, 1968)

Holloway, John, *The Story of the Night* (London, 1961)

Mack, Maynard, *Killing the King: Three Studies in Shakespeare's Tragic Structure* (London, 1972)

Critical Studies: Hamlet

Muir, Kenneth, *Shakespeare's Tragic Sequence* (London, 1979)
        Shakespeare the Professional and Related Studies (London, 1972)
Styan, J. L., *Shakespeare's Stagecraft* (Cambridge, 1967)

Studies of Hamlet

Alexander, Nigel, *Poison, Play, and Duel: A Study in 'Hamlet'* (London, 1971)
Calderwood, James L., *To be and Not to Be – Negation and Melodrama in 'Hamlet'* (New York, 1983)
Charney, Maurice, *Style in 'Hamlet'* (Princeton, N.J., 1969)
Dodsworth, Martin, *Hamlet Closely Observed* (Athlone, 1985)
Jump, J. D., *Shakespeare, 'Hamlet': A Casebook* (London, 1968)
Knights, L. C., *An Approach to 'Hamlet'* (London, 1960)
Levin, Harry, *The Question of 'Hamlet'* (New York, 1959)
Prosser, Eleanor A., *'Hamlet' and Revenge* (Stanford, 1967)
Scofield, Martin, *The Ghosts of 'Hamlet': The Play and Modern Writers* (Cambridge, 1980)
Waldock, A. J. A., *'Hamlet': A Study in Critical Method* (Cambridge, 1931)

READ MORE IN PENGUIN

In every corner of the world, on every subject under the sun, Penguin represents quality and variety – the very best in publishing today.

For complete information about books available from Penguin – including Puffins, Penguin Classics and Arkana – and how to order them, write to us at the appropriate address below. Please note that for copyright reasons the selection of books varies from country to country.

In the United Kingdom: Please write to *Dept. EP, Penguin Books Ltd, Bath Road, Harmondsworth, West Drayton, Middlesex UB7 ODA*

In the United States: Please write to *Consumer Sales, Penguin Putnam Inc., P.O. Box 999, Dept. 17109, Bergenfield, New Jersey 07621-0120.* VISA and MasterCard holders call 1-800-253-6476 to order Penguin titles

In Canada: Please write to *Penguin Books Canada Ltd, 10 Alcorn Avenue, Suite 300, Toronto, Ontario M4V 3B2*

In Australia: Please write to *Penguin Books Australia Ltd, P.O. Box 257, Ringwood, Victoria 3134*

In New Zealand: Please write to *Penguin Books (NZ) Ltd, Private Bag 102902, North Shore Mail Centre, Auckland 10*

In India: Please write to *Penguin Books India Pvt Ltd, 210 Chiranjiv Tower, 43 Nehru Place, New Delhi 110 019*

In the Netherlands: Please write to *Penguin Books Netherlands bv, Postbus 3507, NL-1001 AH Amsterdam*

In Germany: Please write to *Penguin Books Deutschland GmbH, Metzlerstrasse 26, 60594 Frankfurt am Main*

In Spain: Please write to *Penguin Books S. A., Bravo Murillo 19, 1° B, 28015 Madrid*

In Italy: Please write to *Penguin Italia s.r.l., Via Benedetto Croce 2, 20094 Corsico, Milano*

In France: Please write to *Penguin France, Le Carré Wilson, 62 rue Benjamin Baillaud, 31500 Toulouse*

In Japan: Please write to *Penguin Books Japan Ltd, Kaneko Building, 2-3-25 Koraku, Bunkyo-Ku, Tokyo 112*

In South Africa: Please write to *Penguin Books South Africa (Pty) Ltd, Private Bag X14, Parkview, 2122 Johannesburg*

READ MORE IN PENGUIN

CRITICAL STUDIES

Described by *The Times Educational Supplement* as 'admirable' and 'superb', Penguin Critical Studies is a specially developed series of critical essays on the major works of literature for use by students in universities, colleges and schools.

Titles published or in preparation include:

The Poetry of William Blake
Dickens' Major Novels
Doctor Faustus
Emma and Persuasion
Frankenstein
Great Expectations
The Great Gatsby
Heart of Darkness
The Poetry of Gerard
  Manley Hopkins
Jude the Obscure
The Poetry of Keats
Mansfield Park
The Mayor of Casterbridge
The Mill on the Floss
Paradise Lost

The Poetry of Alexander Pope
A Portrait of the Artist as a
  Young Man
Rosencrantz and Guildenstern
  are Dead
Sense and Sensibility
The Poetry of Shelley
Sons and Lovers
Tennyson
Tess of the D'Urbervilles
To the Lighthouse
The Waste Land
Wordsworth
Wuthering Heights
The Poetry of W. B. Yeats

LITERARY CRITICISM

The Penguin History of Literature

Published in ten volumes, *The Penguin History of Literature* is a superb critical survey of the English and American literature covering fourteen centuries, from the Anglo-Saxons to the present, and written by some of the most distinguished academics in their fields.

Epistemology of the Closet Eve Kosofsky Sedgwick

Through her brilliant interpretation of the readings of Henry James, Melville, Nietzsche, Proust and Oscar Wilde, Eve Kosofsky Sedgwick shows how questions of sexual definition are at the heart of every form of representation in this century. 'A signal event in the history of late-twentieth-century gay studies. I don't feel so remunerated, so challenged, so moved, by anything else I've read in the field' – Wayne Koestenbaum

The Anatomy of Criticism Northrop Frye

'Here is a book fundamental enough to be entitled *Principia Critica*', wrote one critic. Northrop Frye's seminal masterpiece was the first work to argue for the status of literary criticism as a science: a true discipline whose techniques and approaches could systematically – and beneficially – be evaluated, quantified and categorized.

Slip-Shod Sibyls Germaine Greer

'The premise of contemporary feminism has been a sentimental illusion from the start. Greer rightly turns her artillery against it, and from a startling new position: she maintains that ... it is coddling and condescending overpraise, not simple obstruction, that has done most damage to women poets' – *Observer*

Dangerous Pilgrimages Malcolm Bradbury

'This capacious book tracks Henry James from New England to Rye; Evelyn Waugh to a Hollywood as grotesque as he expected; Gertrude Stein to Spain to be mistaken for a bishop; Oscar Wilde to a rickety stage in Leadsville, Colorado ... The textbook on the the transatlantic theme' – *Guardian*

READ MORE IN PENGUIN

LITERARY CRITICISM

A Lover's Discourse   Roland Barthes

'*A Lover's Discourse* . . . may be the most detailed, painstaking anatomy of desire we are ever likely to see or need again . . . The book is an ecstatic celebration of love and language and . . . readers interested in either or both . . . will enjoy savouring its rich and dark delights' – *Washington Post Book World*

The New Pelican Guide to English Literature   Edited by Boris Ford

The indispensable critical guide to English and American literature in nine volumes, erudite yet accessible. From the ages of Chaucer and Shakespeare, via Georgian satirists and Victorian social critics, to the leading writers of the twentieth century, all literary life is here.

The Structure of Complex Words   William Empson

'Twentieth-century England's greatest critic after T. S. Eliot, but whereas Eliot was the high priest, Empson was the *enfant terrible* . . . *The Structure of Complex Words* is one of the linguistic masterpieces of the epoch, finding in the feel and tone of our speech whole sedimented social histories' – *Guardian*

The Art of Fiction   David Lodge

The articles with which David Lodge entertained and enlightened readers of the *Independent on Sunday* and the *Washington Post* are now revised, expanded and collected together in book form. 'Agreeable and highly instructive . . . a real treat' – *Sunday Telegraph*

Vamps and Tramps   Camille Paglia

'Paglia is a genuinely unconventional thinker . . . In this collection she is best on homosexual politics, the betrayal of feminism and the sterility of American academe. Taken as a whole, the book gives an exceptionally interesting perspective on the last thirty years of intellectual life in America, and is, in its wacky way, a celebration of passion and the pursuit of truth' – *Sunday Telegraph*

READ MORE IN PENGUIN

REFERENCE

The Penguin Dictionary of Literary Terms and Literary Theory
J. A. Cuddon

'Scholarly, succinct, comprehensive and entertaining, this is an important book, an indispensable work of reference. It draws on the literature of many languages and quotes aptly and freshly from our own' – *The Times Educational Supplement*

The Penguin Spelling Dictionary

What are the plurals of *octopus* and *rhinoceros*? What is the difference between *stationery* and *stationary*? And how about *annex* and *annexe*, *agape* and *Agape*? This comprehensive new book, the fullest spelling dictionary now available, provides the answers.

The Roget's Thesaurus of English Words and Phrases
Betty Kirkpatrick (ed.)

This new edition of Roget's classic work, now brought up to date for the nineties, will increase anyone's command of the English language. Fully cross-referenced, it includes synonyms of every kind (formal or colloquial, idiomatic and figurative) for almost 900 headings. It is a must for writers and utterly fascinating for any English speaker.

The Penguin Dictionary of English Idioms
Daphne M. Gulland and David G. Hinds-Howell

The English language is full of pitfalls for the foreign student – but the most common problem lies in understanding and using the vast array of idioms. *The Penguin Dictionary of English Idioms* is uniquely designed to stimulate understanding and familiarity by explaining the meanings and origins of idioms and giving examples of typical usage.

The Penguin Wordmaster Dictionary
Martin H. Manser and Nigel D. Turton

This dictionary puts the pleasure back into word-seeking. Every time you look at a page you get a bonus – a panel telling you everything about a particular word or expression. It is, therefore, a dictionary to be read as well as used for its concise and up-to-date definitions.

READ MORE IN PENGUIN

REFERENCE

Medicines: A Guide for Everybody Peter Parish

Now in its seventh edition and completely revised and updated, this bestselling guide is written in ordinary language for the ordinary reader yet will prove indispensable to anyone involved in health care – nurses, pharmacists, opticians, social workers and doctors.

Media Law Geoffrey Robertson QC and Andrew Nichol

Crisp and authoritative surveys explain the up-to-date position on defamation, obscenity, official secrecy, copyright and confidentiality, contempt of court, the protection of privacy and much more.

The Penguin Careers Guide
Anna Alston and Anne Daniel; Consultant Editor: Ruth Miller

As the concept of a 'job for life' wanes, this guide encourages you to think broadly about occupational areas as well as describing day-to-day work and detailing the latest developments and qualifications such as NVQs. Special features include possibilities for working part-time and job-sharing, returning to work after a break and an assessment of the current position of women.

The Penguin Dictionary of Troublesome Words Bill Bryson

Why should you avoid discussing the *weather conditions*? Can a married woman be celibate? Why is it eccentric to talk about the aroma of a cowshed? A straightforward guide to the pitfalls and hotly disputed issues in standard written English.

The Penguin Dictionary of Musical Performers Arthur Jacobs

In this invaluable companion volume to *The Penguin Dictionary of Music* Arthur Jacobs has brought together the names of over 2,500 performers. Music is written by composers, yet it is the interpreters who bring it to life; in this comprehensive book they are at last given their due.

READ MORE IN PENGUIN

CRITICAL STUDIES

Described by *The Times Educational Supplement* as 'admirable' and 'superb', Penguin Critical Studies is a specially developed series of critical essays on the major works of literature for use by students in universities, colleges and schools.

Titles published or in preparation include:

SHAKESPEARE

As You Like It
Hamlet
Julius Caesar
King Lear
The Merchant of Venice
A Midsummer Night's Dream
Much Ado about Nothing
Othello
Romeo and Juliet
Shakespeare's History Plays
The Taming of the Shrew
The Tempest
Twelfth Night
The Winter's Tale

CHAUCER

Chaucer
The Pardoner's Tale
The Prologue to
 The Canterbury Tales